The Ultimate Law School Application Guide

UniAdmissions

ISBN 978-1-912557-11-0

Published by *RAR Medical Services Limited*
www.uniadmissions.co.uk
info@uniadmissions.co.uk
Tel: 0208 068 0438

The Ultimate Law School Application Guide

Aiden Ang

Dr Rohan Agarwal

UniAdmissions

About the Authors

Aiden graduated from Peterhouse, Cambridge, with a First Class Honours Law degree and has tutored Oxbridge law applicants at *UniAdmissions* for two years.

Aiden is a trainee solicitor at a top US firm in London and he likes to travel and run outdoors in his spare time. He has a keen interest in helping out students with application advice as he believes that students should get all the help they need in order to succeed in their applications.

Rohan is the **Director of Operations** at *UniAdmissions* and is responsible for its technical and commercial arms. He graduated from Gonville and Caius College, Cambridge and is a fully qualified doctor. Over the last five years, he has tutored hundreds of successful Oxbridge and Medical applicants. He has also authored twenty books on admissions tests and interviews.

Rohan has taught physiology to undergraduates and interviewed medical school applicants for Cambridge. He has published research on bone physiology and writes education articles for the Independent and Huffington Post. In his spare time, Rohan enjoys playing the piano and table tennis.

INTRODUCTION

Well done on taking you first step to a career in a fantastic field. Law school is highly competitive and you are generally competing with the best of the best for a spot in the top institutions. Many students desire to study law for various reasons – be it the fact that it is a prestigious academic subject, the good job prospects, or the rather cliché fact that they have watched Suits or CSI.

Law schools not only look out for pure academic ability in the form of good grades, they also look out for effective writing skills, an ability to think critically, and very importantly a passion for the subject. Many students think that to study law you have to aspire to be a lawyer – this is not true! Law is an academic subject, not a vocational subject such as medicine, and many students who study law go on to work in different fields that are unrelated to law, such as politics and international organisations.

This book aims to set out the steps involved in applying for law school, and how to tackle each step with confidence and fully prepare for the lengthy and tedious application process. Thousands of applicants are successful in attaining a spot in a prestigious law school each year, and there is no reason why you should not as long as you work hard in preparing for the admissions process.

This book covers each of the steps required in making a successful application, guiding you through the application process. In reading the book, you can benefit from the experience of the many successful applicants and specialist tutors who contributed to the resources. You can read the book as a whole in order to gain a perspective on the entire application process, or focus on individual sections to build specific skills.

| Getting the Grades | Personal Statement | Admissions Tests (LNAT/CLT/Nil) | Interviews (Oxbridge Only) |

This book contains elements from four titles in the *UniAdmissions Ultimate Guide* book series. It is designed to be an introduction to the law school application process rather than a comprehensive guide for each component.

You are highly advised to look at each individual book for more advice, strategies and questions when it comes to actually sitting the exam. You can get free copies of all of the books below by flick to the back:

➢ *LNAT Mock Papers*
➢ *The Ultimate LNAT Guide*
➢ *The Ultimate Oxbridge Interview Guide*
➢ *The Ultimate Cambridge Law Test Guide*
➢ *The Ultimate UCAS Personal Statement Guide*

PERSONAL STATEMENTS

Personal Statement

The personal statement can be a very important aspect of the law school admission process, especially when some universities do not use any admissions tests or interviews at all (e.g. LSE). This means that for such universities you will only be able to impress them based on your grades and your personal statement. This makes the personal statement highly important and you want to make sure your personal statement is as error-free as possible and shows a strong desire to study law as an academic subject and how you can demonstrate your interest in the subject.

Even for universities that have additional admissions tests and/or interviews, the personal statement is sometimes effectively used as an entry-barrier in order for the universities to select candidates for the interview on top of your academic grades. A personal statement can make or break a candidate's chance of admission, no matter or good their grades are (e.g. a candidate with 4 A*s might lose out to a candidate with 1 A* if the latter candidate has a much better personal statement). Hence, it is crucial for you to spend a lot of time crafting your personal statement and making it as individualised as possible in order to stand out from the thousands of personal statements that tutors have to read each year.

The Process

You have to submit your university application via the UCAS online portal – you are only allowed to submit one personal statement to all five universities, so make sure your personal statement only talks about why you want to apply for law and not any particular university (unless in the rare case where you only intend to apply for one university, but this is not advisable due to the risks involved).

For example, even if you strongly prefer to apply for either Oxford or Cambridge, you should not allude to this in your personal statement (e.g. by talking about the collegiate system or the small class ratio) as the other universities might get the idea that you are not as interested in applying to them.

You get to pick up to five choices, and it is advisable for all five of your choices to be for law since you are only allowed to submit one personal statement for all five of your choices. Some universities might give you an offer right off the bat, but other universities tend to have an additional test or interview requirement.

> **Top Tip**
> If you're applying to Cambridge, you'll have to complete an additional form called the SAQ where you'll have the opportunity to include a personal statement specifically for Cambridge

The Timescale

The general UCAS deadline is 15 January, but Oxbridge has a much earlier deadline of 15 October (previous year), so do take note of this earlier deadline if you wish to apply for Oxbridge. There are also additional deadlines if admissions tests and interviews are involved – for example, a university may stipulate that you should do the LNAT by a certain date, these are all subject to the university and you should keep track of the correspondence with your university so as to not miss any deadlines.

What are the Requirements?

➤ Maximum 4000 characters
➤ Maximum 47 lines
➤ Submitted by the early deadline – 15 October if applying to Oxbridge
➤ Submitted by the general deadline if applying for all other universities

What do Admissions Tutors look for?

Grades

This is probably by the most important element for a law school application. Remember – law is an academically rigorous subject, with heavy demands when it comes to reading and understanding complex concepts. Hence, good grades are always a good indicator for tutors when it comes to figuring out whether a candidate has the academic aptitude for studying law and whether they will be able to cope with the demanding curriculum. Most top universities will usually demand at least an AAB at A levels (this is subject to change every year), with Oxbridge typically demanding A*AA. Universities (particularly Oxbridge) also look at traditional A level subjects more favourably as they are deemed more academically rigorous. This does not mean that doing a less traditional subject (e.g. business, psychology) will reduce your chances of admission, this just means that tutors are fair and do take into account the fact that traditional subjects such as the hard sciences or the traditional arts subjects are harder to score well in. Hence, the main priority of an applicant is to always make sure they have the pre-requisite grades to apply for law school.

An interest in law

This is arguably the next most important element of the law school admission process. This can be demonstrated in various ways – some applicants have done wide further reading about law-related topics, others have done law-related work experience such as shadowing a barrister or volunteering in free legal clinics. There is no standard way of showing an interest in law, and some candidates do impress by showing their interest in law by more unorthodox manners (e.g. talking about their experience with the legal system and how it sparked their interest in the law). Whatever you do, make sure you are genuine in showing your interest in law in your personal statement and do not make up facts that you cannot support – a personal statement that comes across as rehearsed and incredible will not stand a good chance of gaining admission.

Good performance in admissions tests/interviews

For universities that use admissions tests such as the LNAT or the Cambridge Law Test, this can play a huge factor in deciding whether a candidate has a good chance of gaining admission. This is used as an additional tool on top of your grades and personal statement – there are so many students with stellar grades competing for limited spots in top law schools, sometimes a personal statement is simply insufficient to weed out the very best candidates. Admissions tests and/or interviews are basically designed to test a candidate's raw legal ability – they always emphasise that no prior legal knowledge is needed, but a candidate will not be doing him or herself a favour by going into these tests or interviews unprepared. Sometimes, a good score on the admissions tests and/or a good performance at the interview can counteract weaker grades, hence grades are not the be all and end all, although they are highly important.

Application Timeline

Component	Deadline	Component	Deadline
Research Courses	June + July	Expert Checks	Mid-September
Start Brainstorming	Start of August	Submit to School	Late September
Complete 1st Draft	Mid-August	Submit to UCAS	Before 15th October (Oxbridge deadline)
Complete Final Draft	End of August	Submit to UCAS	Before 15th January (General deadline)

1) Researching Courses

Even though law may seem the same for different universities, there are subtle differences you should take note of and the best way of finding out is to do your due diligence by researching the courses online or by attending open days in the respective universities if possible. For example, Cambridge organises a Sixth Form Law Conference each year, and plenty of other universities organise subject open days to give sixth form students a flavour of what to expect in a law undergraduate course.

Some universities offer a four-year law degree, which one year is usually spent abroad learning law in a different jurisdiction (e.g. Law with French Law, Law with American Law). This might appeal to students who wish to have a more international education and have a genuine interest in an international legal career, or students who have a particular language skill and wish to utilise that during their law studies. These courses will be very specific and they will tend to have an additional section for you to fill up in your UCAS application, so you do not have to worry about having to explain why you want to do the additional year abroad in your personal statement – just focus on why you want to study law in general in your personal statement as it is unlikely for all five of your choices to include a study abroad option.

You might also want to pick your universities based on the modules they are able to offer – e.g. some universities may have more elective choices than others due to the availability of professors, and if you have a particular niche interest such as in IP law for example this might be a deciding factor in choosing your five universities to apply to.

Of course, the location of a university may be important for you as well – being in London for example might mean easy access to the courts, law firms and chambers, but it might also mean a higher living cost as well as a different form of student life compared to more collegiate universities.

2) Start Brainstorming

At this stage, you will have narrowed down your subject interests and should be certain that you're applying for law (if you're not then check out our "*Ultimate Personal Statement Guide*" for other subjects).

A good way to start a thought process which will eventually lead to a personal statement is by simply listing all of your ideas, why you are interested in your course and the pros and cons between different universities. If there are particular modules which capture your interest that are common across several of your university choices, do not be afraid to include this in your personal statement. This will show not only that you have a real interest in your chosen subject, but also that you have taken the time to do your research.

3) Complete First Draft

This will not be the final personal statement that you submit. In all likelihood, your personal statement will go through multiple revisions and re-drafts before it is ready for submission. In most cases, the final statement is greatly different from the first draft.

The purpose of completing a rough draft early is so that you can spot major errors early. It is easy to go off on a tangent when writing a personal statement, with such things not being made obvious until somebody else reads it. The first draft will show the applicant which areas need more attention, what is missing and what needs to be removed altogether.

4) Re-Draft

This will probably be the first time at which you receive any real feedback on your Personal Statement. Obvious errors will be spotted, and any outrageous claims that sound good in your head, but are unclear or dubious will be obvious to the reader at this stage.

It is important to take advice from family and friends, however with a pinch of salt. Remember that the admissions tutor will be a stranger and not familiar with the applicant's personality.

5) Expert Check

This should be completed by the time you return for your final year at school/college. Once the final year has started, it is wise to get as many experts (teachers and external tutors) to read through the draft personal statement as possible

Again, you should take all advice with a pinch of salt. At the end of the day, this is your UCAS application and although your teachers' opinions are valuable, they are not the same as that of the admissions tutors. In schools that see many law and Oxbridge applications, many teachers believe there is a correct 'format' to personal statements, and may look at your statement like 'number' in the sea of applications that are processed by the school. There is no 'format' to successful personal statements, as each statement should be **personal** to you.

At schools that do not see many Oxbridge/law applications, the opposite may be true. Many applicants are coerced into applying to universities and for courses which their teachers judge them likely to be accepted for. It is your responsibility to ensure that the decisions you make are your own, and you have the conviction to follow through with your decisions.

6) Submit to School

Ideally, you will have some time off before submitting your statement for the internal UCAS deadline. This is important because it'll allow you to look at your final personal statement with a fresh perspective before submitting it. You'll also be able to spot any errors that you initially missed. You should submit your personal statement and UCAS application to your school on time for the internal deadline. This ensures that your school has enough time to complete your references.

7) Submit to UCAS

That's it! Take some time off from university applications for a few days, have some rest and remember that you still have A levels/IB exams to get through (and potentially admissions tests and interviews).

Getting Started

The personal statement is an amalgamation of all your hard work throughout both secondary school and your other extracurricular activities. It is right to be apprehensive about starting your application and so here are a few tips to get you started…

General Rules

If you meet the minimum academic requirements then it is with the personal statement that your application to university will be made or broken. With many applicants applying with identical GCSE and A-level results (if you're a gap year student) the personal statement is your chance to really stand out and let your personality shine through. As such there is no concrete formula to follow when writing the personal statement and indeed every statement is different in its own right. Therefore throughout this chapter you will find many principles for you to adopt and interpret as you see fit whilst considering a few of these introductory general rules.

Firstly: **space is extremely limited**; as previously mentioned a maximum of 4000 characters in 47 lines. Before even beginning the personal statement utilise all available space on the UCAS form. For example do not waste characters listing exam results when they can be entered in the corresponding fields in the qualifications section of the UCAS form.

Secondly: always remember **it easier to reduce the word count** than increase it with meaningful content when editing. Be aware that is not practical to perfect your personal statement in just one sitting. Instead write multiple drafts starting with one substantially exceeding the word limit but containing all your ideas. As such starting early is key to avoid later time pressure as you approach the deadline. Remember this is your opportunity to put onto paper what makes you the best and a cut above the rest – you should enjoy writing the personal statement!

Lastly and most importantly: **your statement is just one of hundreds that a tutor will read**. Tutors are only human after all and their interpretation of your personal statement can be influenced by many things. So get on their good side and always be sympathetic to the reader, make things plain and easy to read, avoid contentious subjects and never target your personal statement at one particular university (unless you're only applying there!).

When Should I Start?

Although it might sound like a cliché, the earlier you start writing, the easier you make the process. Starting early helps you in four key ways:

1) The most important reason to start early is that it is the **best way to analyse your application**. Many students start writing their personal statement then realise, for example, that they haven't done enough work experience, or that their extra reading isn't focused enough. *By starting early, you give yourself the chance to change this.* Over the summer, catch up on your weak areas to give yourself plenty to say in the final version.

2) **You give yourself more time for revisions.** You can improve your personal statement by showing it to as many people as possible to get their feedback. With an earlier start, you have more time to modify, thus improving the final result.

3) **Steadier pace.** Starting early gives you the flexibility of working at a steadier pace – perhaps just an hour or so per week. If you start later, you will have to spend much longer on it – probably some full days – reducing the time you have for the rest of your work and importantly for unwinding, too.

4) **You can finish it earlier.** If you start early, you can finish early too. This gives you time to change focus and start preparing for the LNAT, Cambridge Law Test (if needed), and for your interviews (if any), which are usually conducted in December for Oxbridge (or earlier for international applicants doing their interviews abroad).

What people think is best:

What is actually best:

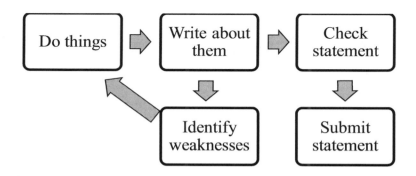

Taking your First Steps

A journey of a thousand miles starts with a single step...

As you may have already experienced, the hardest step of a big project is the first step. It's easy to *plan* to start something, but when it *actually* comes to writing the first words, what do you do? As you stare at the 47-line blank page in front of you, how can you fill it? You wonder if you've even done that many things in life. You think of something, but realise it probably isn't good enough, delete it and start over again. Sound familiar?

There is another way. The reason it is hard is because you judge your thoughts against the imagined finished product. So don't begin by writing full, perfectly polished sentences. Don't be a perfectionist. Begin with lists, spider diagrams, ideas, rambling. Just put some ideas onto paper and **write as much as possible** – it's easy to trim down afterwards if it's too long, and generally doing it this way gives the best content. Aim to improve gradually from start to finish in little steps each time.

Doing your Research

The two most important things you need to establish are: ***What course?*** and ***What University?***

If you're unsure of where to begin, success with the personal statement begins with preparation and research.

Your choice of university is entirely personal and similar to your course choice; it needs to be somewhere that you are going to enjoy studying. Remember that where you end up will form a substantial part of your life. This could mean going to a university with a rich, active nightlife or one with strict academic prowess or perhaps one that dominates in the sporting world. In reality each university offers its own unique experience and hence the best approach is to attend as many open days as feasibly possible. At which you will have the opportunity to meet some of your potential tutors, talk to current students (who offer the most honest information) and of course tour the facilities.

The best way to prevent future stress is to start researching courses and universities early i.e. 12 months before your apply through UCAS. There is a plethora of information that is freely available online, and if you want something physical to read, you can request free prospectuses from most UK universities. It is important to remember that until you actually submit your UCAS application, **you** are in control. Universities are actively competing against one another for **your** application! When initially browsing, a good place to start is by simply listing courses and universities which interest you, and 2 pros and cons for each. You can then use this to shortlist to a handful of universities that you should then attend open days for.

There are no right choices when it comes to university choices, however there are plenty of wrong choices. You must make sure that the reasons behind your eventual choice are the right ones, and that you do not act on impulse. Whilst your personal statement should not be directed at any particular one of your universities, it should certainly be tailored to the course you are applying for.

With a course in mind and universities short listed your preparation can begin in earnest. Start by ordering **university prospectuses** or logging onto the university's subject specific websites. You should be trying to find the application requirements. Once located there will be a range of information from academic demands including work experience to personal attributes. Firstly at this point **be realistic with the GCSE results you have already achieved and your predicted A-level grades**. If these do not meet the minimum academic requirements a tutor will most likely not even bother reading your personal statement so don't waste a choice.

If you meet all the minimum academic requirements then focus on the other extracurricular aspects. Many prospectuses contain descriptions of ideal candidates with lists of desired personal attributes. Make a list of these for all the universities you are considering applying to. Compile a further list of your own personal attributes along with evidence that supports this claim. Then proceed to pair the points on your personal list with the corresponding requirements from your potential universities. It is important to consider extracurricular requirements from all your potential universities in the interest of forming a **rounded personal statement applicable to all institutions**.

This is a useful technique because one university may not require the same personal attributes as another. Therefore by discussing these attributes in your statement, you can demonstrate a level of ingenuity and personal reflection on the requirements of the course beyond what is listed in the prospectus.

Always remember that the role of the personal statement is to **show that you meet course requirements by using your own personal experiences as evidence**.

Brainstorming

If writing prose is too daunting, start by using our brainstorm template. Write down just three bullet-points for each of the 12 questions below and in only twenty minutes you'll be well on your way!

Why law?

What areas of law interest you the most?

What are your 3 main hobbies and what skills have they developed?

What have you chosen to read outside the A-level syllabus?

Do you have any long-term career ideas/aspirations?

What did you learn from your work experience?

Have you won any prizes or awards?

What is your favourite A-level subject and why?

What are your personal strengths?

Have you attended any courses?

Have you ever held a position of responsibility?

Have you been a part of any projects?

The Writing Process

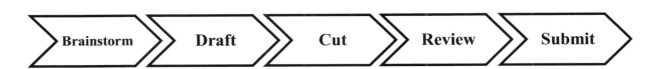

What is the Purpose of your Statement?

An important question to ask yourself before you begin drafting your personal statement is: how will the universities I have applied to use my personal statement? This can dramatically change how you write your personal statement. For some universities that don't interview or conduct any admissions tests, the personal statement is directly bidding for a place on the course.

For universities such as LSE, the personal statement plays a highly important role on top of grades since it is the only thing that the tutors can use to judge your application and determine whether you are deserving of a spot. Since the personal statement will not be used for an interview, you will want to make sure that the personal statement is error-free, conveys your interest to study law strongly, and stands out from the crowd.

For universities that use an admissions test as well, such as the LNAT, the personal statement may not be as important, especially if a candidate scores extremely well in the LNAT in comparison with the other candidates. However, to be on the safe side, you should always ensure that your personal statement is up to scratch, as sometimes it might be the deciding factor between two borderline candidates.

However, if you're applying for Oxbridge, you will have to pass the admission test and the interview as well in order to secure a spot. Hence, you want to make sure that your personal statement will not only stand out from the crowd and give you a good chance of being shortlisted for an interview, but you also have to ensure that whatever is stated in the personal statement can be used during your interview.

Hence, be prepared to be asked challenging and thought-provoking questions based on your personal statement by the interviewers. Make sure you are familiar with the contents of your personal statement, you have done your research beforehand, you have formed an opinion about the legal issues or topics that you have mentioned in your personal statement, and you are prepared to engage in an intense, academic discussion with the interviewers based on your personal statement.

Different tutors have vastly different interview styles – some will base the interview solely on your personal statement, others will use your personal statement as a starting point and go on a tangent based on that, whilst some might not even refer to your personal statement at all! It is highly important to be prepared for all kinds of scenarios, hence make sure you know your personal statement inside out before the interview, ensure that you have done your research adequately, and definitely do not include anything in your personal statement that you cannot support.

Finding the Right Balance

The balance of a personal statement can have a significant effect on the overall message it delivers. Whilst there are no strict rules, there are a few rules of thumb that can help you strike the right balance between all the important sections.

Most importantly, you want to show how you have an interest to study law by giving details on what you have done in order to find out more about law – be it engaging in extra-readings or partaking in law-related activities. You should not be focusing too much on extra-curricular activities that do not bear much relation to the study of law (e.g. spending a few paragraphs talking about your time being the Captain of your football team without actually explaining why this is related to your interest in law).

Remember, application to law school in the UK is very different to the US system, there is less of an emphasis in your extra-curricular activities such as your leadership positions or your sports achievements. The tutors are looking for raw academic talent – hence you need to show how you as a candidate will be able to excel in studying law.

The following template gives a suggestion how to balance the different sections:

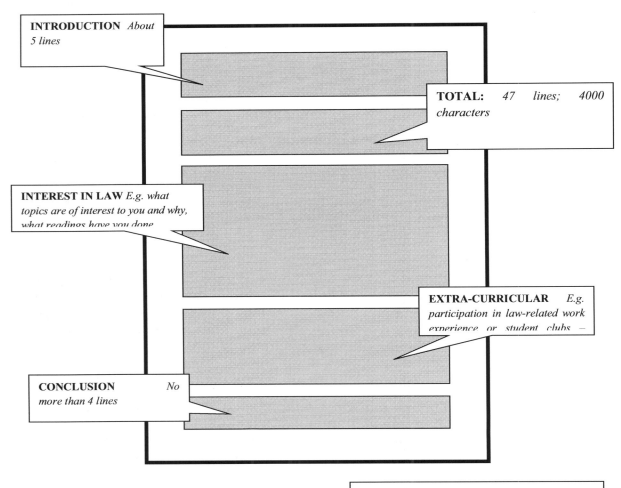

INTRODUCTION *About 5 lines*

TOTAL: *47 lines; 4000 characters*

INTEREST IN LAW *E.g. what topics are of interest to you and why, what readings have you done*

EXTRA-CURRICULAR *E.g. participation in law-related work experience or student clubs –*

CONCLUSION *No more than 4 lines*

TOTAL: *47 lines; 4000 characters*

Structuring Your Statement

This may sound obvious, but many personal statements do not have a good structure. Personal statements are formal pieces of prose written with a clear purpose. Choosing a good structure helps all the important information to shine through clearly and be easily understood by the reader.

The Introduction

The Opening Sentence

Rightly or wrongly, it is likely that your personal statement will be remembered by its opening sentence. It must be something short, sharp, insightful and catch the reader's attention. Remember that admissions tutors will read several hundred personal statements and often their first impression is made by your opening sentence which is why it needs to be eye catching enough to make the tutor sit and pay particular attention to what you have written. It does indeed set the standard for the rest of the personal statement.

If this seems a daunting prospect (as it should!) then here are a few pointers to get you started:
➢ Avoid using overused words like "passionate", "deeply fascinating" and "devotion".
➢ Avoid using clichéd quotes like "I have always been fascinated with the intracies of the UK legal system".
➢ If you are going to use a quote then put some effort into researching an obscure yet particular powerful – don't forget to include a reference.
➢ Draw on your own personal experiences to produce something both original and eye-catching.

In many ways it is best that you save writing your opening statement till last; that way you can assess the tone of the rest of your work but also write something that will not be repeated elsewhere.

If you are really stuck with where to begin try writing down a memory and then explain how it has affected your relationship with your subject.

Whilst the opening statement is important, it is not something to stress about. Although a strong opening statement can make the personal statement; a bad one rarely breaks it.

Why law?

The introduction should answer the most important question of all – **why law?**

*Why do **YOU** want to study law?*

It bears repeating that you should be talking about why you want to study law as an **academic subject**, not necessarily why you want to be a 'lawyer'. 'Lawyer' is a very generic and misleading term as there are many different types of lawyers – be it a barrister, solicitor, or legal academic. Hence, even if you are dead set on a particular career path, be accurate and precise in talking about the kind of lawyer you aspire to be. But most importantly, focus on why law as a subject is interesting to you.

➢ **Intellectually stimulating:** Many students state this reason, as law is a complex subject that demands a good understanding of many different concepts
➢ **Personal experience:** Some students might talk about their personal experience with the law – e.g. experiencing a criminal trial or helping out a friend in a legal dispute
➢ **Human rights:** Many students have an interest in law because of the human rights element to it – e.g. immigration law, family law and international law are all heavily intertwined with human rights
➢ **Career:** This is a perfectly legitimate motivation for studying law, and some students like to focus on the more commercial side of law and why it interests them (e.g. company law, commercial law)
➢ **Versatile and flexible subject:** Some students appreciate the fact that law is a versatile subject that covers elements of sociology, psychology and philosophy

Whichever reason style you choose to go with, or if you have a completely different reason altogether, a good answer always has a few key features. A good answer to the *"why law"* question will always allow the examiners to sense a genuine motivation to study law and demonstrate sufficient evidence of an interest in law.

Definitely avoid clichés as they leave an overall bad impression, even if your personal statement is well-written. For example, you should know by now that having watched Suits is not a good enough reason for wanting to study law in university (if that is really your reason, have a rethink about why you want to study law!). Many students also fall into the cliché of wanting to be a defender of human rights and cite the example of Atticus Finch in *To Kill a Mockingbird* or cite Amal Clooney as their role model. These are all valid reasons but they come across as cliché and not genuine.

The *exact* phrase: *"from a young age I have always been interested in"* was used more than 300 times in personal statements in 2013 (data published by UCAS), and substituting "young" for "early" gave an additional 292 statements – these phrases can quickly become boring for admissions tutors to read!

The Main Body

In the rest of your text your aim should be to demonstrate your suitability for the course by exemplifying your knowledge of the course structure and its requirements through personal experience. Again there are no rigorous guidelines on how to do this and it is very much down to your own writing style. Whereas some prefer a strict structure, others go for a more synoptic approach, but always remember to be consistent in order to achieve a flowing, easy to read personal statement.

This point ties in closely with writing style. You want one that the tutor will find pleasing to read; and as everyone prefers different styles the only way to assess yours accurately is to show your drafts to as many people as possible. That includes, teachers, parents, friends, siblings, grandparents – the more the better, don't be afraid to show it round!

Despite the lack of a standardised writing method, there is of course a list of standard content to include. In general you are trying to convey your academic, professional and personal suitability for the course to the tutor. This needs to be reiterated whilst demonstrating clear, exemplified knowledge of the course structure and its demands. The biggest problem then in achieving these goals, with all the other candidates also trying to convey the same information, is in producing an original personal statement and remaining unique.

The easiest way to overcome this is to integrate your own personal experiences, reflections and emotions – both demonstrating passion and insight. More practically, it is a good idea to split the main body into two or three paragraphs, in order to avoid writing one big giant boring monologue.

Part One: This should cover why you are suited for law. This will include your main academic interests, future ambitions and what makes law right for you. It is a good idea for you to read up the course syllabuses, and find something that catches your interest above others. If you have read anything outside of the A-level/IB syllabus related to your chosen course which has inspired you then this is the place to mention it.

Part Two: This section should still be about why you're suited to your chosen course with a particular focus on work experience. If you've had to overcome any significant challenges in life and wish to include these in your personal statement, then this is normally the best place to do so. Similarly, any relevant prizes & competitions should be included here. However, it is important to remember not to simply list things. Ensure that you follow through by describing in detail what you have learned from any experiences mentioned.

Part Three: This is the smallest part of the main body and is all about extra-curricular activities. It is easy to get carried away in this section and make outrageous claims e.g. claim to be a mountain climber if all you have ever climbed is a hill at the end your street etc. Lying is not worth the risk given that your interviewer may share the same hobby that you claim to be an expert in!

Avoid making empty statements by backing things up with facts. For example: *'I enjoy reading, playing sports and watching TV',* is a poor sentence and tells the reader nothing. The applicant enjoys reading, so what? Which sports? Doesn't everyone like watching TV? If the applicant is in a sports team, or plays a particular sport recreationally with friends then they should name the sport and describe what their role is. Likewise, the applicant should actually describe how their hobbies relate to them as a person and ideally their subject.

What to Include

Still a little stumped? Here is a summary of a few useful pointers to get you started:

➢ **Extra-readings** – law is a heavily reading-intensive subject and showing that you have done extra-readings in order to discover why you are interested in law and engage in a particular topic will always put you in a good light and show your suitability in studying law as an academic subject. Make sure you are familiar with whatever you include, especially if there is an interview involved – you do not want to be caught in the awkward situation whereby the interview asks about the book you have mentioned and you have completely forgot what it is about!

➢ **Any relevant competitions/essay prizes** – Winning certain competitions or prizes such as a book prize, an essay prize or a debating competition can be highly relevant and impressive in your law application, as they show that you are good at arguing your point and analysing topics in a critical manner – important attributes law tutors are looking out for. Winning a sports competition may be less relevant in comparison, as they do not really link back to why you are suited to study law.

➢ **Personal interests within the field of study** – This is a really good opportunity to show off your own genuine interest within the subject field. Try to mention a recent article or paper, one that isn't too contentious but is still not that well known to show depth of reading.

➢ **Personal attributes** – exemplify these through your own personal experiences and opinions. As mentioned previously many courses will list "desired" personal attributes in their prospectus - you must include these as a minimum in your personal statement. Try to add others of your own choice that you think are relevant to the subject in order to achieve originality.

➢ **Academic awards/achievements** – even though the tutors already know your grades, it may be worthwhile to talk about what you have learned about in your subjects and why they might have inspired you to study law (e.g. how history has shaped your essay-writing skills and argumentative abilities), and being top in your class for a subject may show a heightened level of academic ability which will impress the tutors

Together, discussion of all these points can demonstrate reasoned consideration for the course you have applied for. This is particularly appealing for a tutor to read as it shows a higher level of thinking by giving your own reflection on the course requirements.

The Conclusion

The conclusion of your personal statement should be more about leaving a good final impression than conferring any actual information. If you have something useful to say about your interest and desire to study law, you shouldn't be waiting until the very end to say it!

Admissions tutors will read hundreds of personal statements every year, and after about the fifth one all start looking very much the same. You should try to make your statement different so it stands out amongst the rest. As the conclusion is the last thing the admissions tutor will read, it can leave a lasting influence (good or bad!) The purpose of a conclusion is to tie up the entire statement in two or three sentences.

A good conclusion should not include any new information, as this should be in the main body. However, you also need to avoid repeating what you have said earlier in your personal statement. This would be both a waste of characters and frustrating for the tutor. Instead it is better to put into context what you have already written and therefore make an effort to keep your conclusion relatively short – no more than 4 lines.

The conclusion is a good opportunity to draw on all the themes you have introduced throughout your personal statement to form a final overall character image to leave the tutor with. Unless there is anything especially extraordinary or outrageous in the main body of your personal statement; the tutor is likely to remember you by your introduction and conclusion. The conclusion therefore is a good place to leave an inspiring final sentence for the tutor.

Some students will make a mention in here about their career plans, picking up on something they have observed in work experience or have encountered during reading. This can be a good strategy as it shows you're using your current knowledge to guide your future aspirations. If you do this, try to do so with an open mind, suggesting areas of interest but being careful not to imply you are less interested in others.

Once again, do not place too much emphasis on talking about your career plan as this is not what the tutor is looking out for, although it may be useful to show your genuine interest in studying law. It might be more useful to conclude by showing how you find law interesting because of certain topics that intrigue you, and the fact that a law degree will provide a good intellectual training for any career path that you might embark on in the future, be it law or non-law.

It is important to avoid sounding too arrogant here and over selling yourself. Instead adopt a phrase looking forward in time – perhaps expressing your excitement and enthusiasm in meeting the demands of your course requirements, or looking even further ahead, the demands of your career. For example, consider a phrase like: *'driven by my love of law, I am sure that I will be a successful lawyer and take full advantage of all opportunities should this application be successful'* rather than *'I think I should be accepted because I am very enthusiastic and will work hard'*. The sentiment behind both of these statements is positive, however the second sounds juvenile whereas the first is aspirational, confident and yet humble.

FURTHER READING

Perhaps one of the best ways to show a genuine interest in law is to show that you have done further reading about area(s) of law that interests you. After all, law as a subject has a heavy emphasis on independent learning and further reading, and you may have heard the rumours about students having to read hundreds of pages every week as part of their curriculum. The rumours are true – you cannot shy away from reading copious amounts of text if you wish to take up law!

You do not strictly have to read about the law itself, in fact we would not expect sixth form students to be reading up about the statutes and case law – they are perhaps a bit too dense and students without a law background would not be able to fully understand and grasp the concepts (that is what law school is for after all).

You can easily show an interest in law even if you only read fiction books – in fact, fiction books can be a good starting point in demonstrating how you started to develop an interest in law. For example, you might have read a book by Jodi Picoult about a mother's struggle with having a baby with brittle bone disease and she was embroiled in a law suit as she was falsely accused of child abuse. Picking up on certain legal issues form fiction novels can be an interesting way of showing how you developed an interest in law from a young age, and will certainly stand out from the crowd if you manage to find an interesting and novel example.

Of course, another good way of showing an interest in law is to keep up with current affairs, and needless to say the latest happenings in our political climate provide good fodder for thinking about certain legal issues, such as the ongoing Brexit negotiations and migrant rights.

The list of potential readings you can do is certainly non-exhaustive, but here are a few suggestions to get you started:

➢ **The Economist** – provides well-written articles about geo-political issues that might discuss certain legal issues
➢ **Financial Times** – also provides good articles on geo-political issues, with a heavy leaning towards the corporate world, and might be of relevance for students who are more interested in the commercial side of law
➢ **The Guardian, The Times, The Telegraph** etc. – to keep up with current news and it is wise to focus on the legal section of these newspapers for more relevant news
➢ **Fiction Books** involving criminal law, family law or any other area of law that might be of interest to you

BASIC CONCEPTS IN LAW

Criminal Law

This is perhaps an area of law that receives the most publicity and hence most students will think they know something about. However, this is also one of the most complex, controversial, perplexing and confusing areas of law. There are also many related areas to criminal law that are considered separate domains, such as Criminal Procedure and Evidence, as well as Criminology, Sentencing and the Penal System (both are taught as separate subjects in Cambridge).

There are certain hot topics that have been heavily debated in the public arena recently, such as euthanasia (the right to die), joint enterprise (when two or more people are involved in the same crime) and historic sexual abuse cases. These are definitely areas that are usually picked up by students and discussed in great detail because they appear on the news frequently and do raise countless ethical and theoretical questions. However, there are several other areas of criminal law that have caused fervent academic debate, such as defences (e.g. the extent to which being drunk should be a defence to a crime) and recklessness (which crimes will it be enough to show that a defendant was reckless as opposed to having an intention to commit the crime?).

A core tenet of criminal law is that in order for an accused to be convicted of a crime, it must be proved by the prosecution beyond reasonable doubt that he or she had the requisite actus reus (the physical action of the crime, such as the physical act of stealing a wallet) with the accompanying mens rea (the mental element – e.g. the intention of stealing the wallet). The accused will be allowed to raise a defence, for example the defence of lack of mens rea (the accused accidentally took the wallet without the intention of stealing it). For certain crimes such as murder, it may be a defence to show that the accused killed the victim out of self-defence. There are also full defences and partial defences (e.g. it may be a partial defence to show that the accused only attacked the victim because the victim taunted the accused, but this defence will not wholly exonerate the accused unlike self-defence).

Constitutional/Public Law

A recent big constitutional case would be the Brexit decision handed down by the Supreme Court, which was an application brought on behalf of Gina Miller. Constitutional law plays a big part in upholding values such as the rule of law, preserving human rights and ensuring that the government does not abuse its powers – some of these principles may seem really abstract but they play an important role in making England an attractive place to live and do business because of the strong rule of law.

One peculiarity of constitutional law in England is that we lack a written constitution, unlike the US where they have a written constitution that takes an onerous process to amend. There have been countless debates about whether the unwritten constitution works or whether we should adopt a written constitution, and this is where things start to get highly abstract and theoretical at times.

Nonetheless, when judges determine what our constitutional rights are, they tend to infer it from a variety of sources due to the lack of a written constitution, such as the legitimate expectation of a claimant due to established practice, certain treaties and articles that set out basic fundamental rights such as the European Convention on Human Rights (ECHR) (again, this will change following the Brexit decision) or international treaties such as the Geneva Convention. As you can see, human rights are a big part of constitutional law, and this has been governed largely by the Human Rights Act 1998 (HRA 1998), but it has been proposed that this will be repealed and replaced with a Bill of Rights following the Brexit vote as the HRA was largely implemented as a result of the entry into the EU.

Tort Law

Tort Law is perhaps infamous amongst law students for being loaded with cases to remember, as it is so heavily dominated by case law (with a handful of statutory provisions governing certain areas such as the tort of trespass). Tort cases are civil cases – this is not to be confused with the difference between common law and civil law – in this case civil cases refer to private disputes that do not involve the state – hence a private party sues another private party in tort, instead of a prosecutor bringing proceedings against a defendant – this is why criminal cases are almost always named as '*R v. The Defendant*', with 'R' referring to the Crown, whereas tort cases are just between two private parties. In criminal law, where a defendant loses a case he or she will get a penal sentence, a fine, or a community sentence in general, whereas in tort cases the losing party will usually be ordered to pay damages, or be ordered to refrain from doing a particular act such as under an injunction.

Tort cases are generally civil duties that fall outside the realm of contract law – for example an implied duty of care between a professional and a client if there is a lack of an express contract between them. For example, in the situation where you were applying to Cambridge, and needed a reference from your teacher, the teacher is under an implied duty of care to provide an accurate reference for you (he or she is however under no duty to boost your achievements if it is not reflective of your actual achievements!). If a teacher negligently fails to provide an accurate reference – for example if a teacher mistook you for another student that was always skipping class and gave you a bad reference and you failed to get a place in Cambridge, there *might* be a possible tortious claim, but it is subject to the different steps involved in a tortious claim.

The general steps involved in establishing a claim in tort are as follows: i) Duty of care – does the defendant owe a duty of care to the claimant; ii) Breach – has the duty been breach; iii) Causation – was the claimant's loss caused by the defendant's breach; and iv) Loss – has the defendant suffered loss as a result of the breach.

Duty of care

A duty of care can be implied from a professional relationship – e.g. solicitor to client, doctor to patient, but also from a relationship of trust and confidence – e.g. teacher and student, employer and employee. The courts will usually look at the circumstances of the case and decide whether the relationship between the claimant and defendant shows that a duty of care is owed by the defendant.

Breach

It must be shown that the duty of care owed has been breached by the defendant. For example, if a defendant performed his or her job negligently and failed to reach the standard expected of a reasonable professional in the same industry, it will be established that the duty of care has been breached.

Causation

Further, it must be shown that it is the breach that has caused the loss to the claimant. Using the example given above, if the student still would not have gotten into Cambridge despite the wrongly-given reference (e.g. the student did really poorly in the interview or the CLT and even if the reference was spotless the student still would not have been admitted), causation will not be established and a claim will not be available. Sometimes, there might be an intervening cause that breaks the causative chain, for example if the student contracted an illness that impeded his or her performance at the interview, the bad reference will no longer be the causative element behind the unsuccessful outcome.

Loss

Finally, loss has to be established for a claim to exist. In some cases this is straightforward, such as losing a certain amount of money as a result of the negligence of your solicitor. In other cases, such as the example used above, this might be harder to assess – how do we assess the loss of failing to get into Cambridge in monetary terms? Usually claimants will argue this point in terms of loss of future earnings, such as arguing that failing to get into Cambridge will lead to a loss of future job prospects. This is a very controversial area in tort law and the assessment of loss usually boils down to very subjective and speculative judgments.

EXAMPLE CASES

Donoghue v Stevenson (Tort)

This is perhaps one of the most well-known cases for law students, partly due to its unique facts and also partly because of its subsequent importance in tort.

What the case established

Donoghue v Stevenson held that manufacturers could owe a duty of care to consumers under negligence in tort even if the consumer and the manufacturer did not enter into a formal contract (and hence no contractual claim is available).

Facts of the case

The claimant bought a bottle of ginger beer from the defendant, who was a manufacturer of ginger beers. When the claimant drank the bottle of ginger beer, she claimed that there was a snail in the bottle which made her sick as a result.

What the judge(s) said

Lord Atkin famously introduced the 'neighbour principle' in this case, stating that 'the rule that you must love your neighbour became in law that you must not injure your neighbour'. He further held that 'you must take reasonable care to avoid acts or omissions which you could reasonably foresee would be likely to injure your neighbour'. With regards to whom can be regarded as your neighbour, he mentioned that this 'seemed to be persons who were so closely and directly affected by your act that you ought reasonably to have them in contemplation as being so affected when you directed your mind to the acts or omissions which were called into question'.

Why is this case important

This case resulted in the development of the concept of negligence under tort law, where a duty of care can be established under the 'neighbour principle'. This allowed claimants to bring a potential claim under tort for damages they have suffered, which proved particularly useful especially when they could not bring a contractual claim due to a lack of contract.

Hence, a manufacturer could owe a duty of care if they could reasonably foresee that consumers would likely be injured if they were negligent in producing their ginger beers. Consumers fell under the definition of a 'neighbour' as they were so closely and directly affected by the act of the manufacturer that the manufacturer ought to reasonably have the consumers in contemplation as being potentially affected when they thought about their act in question.

The current state of the law

Tort provides protection for consumers in the event that contract fails to provide adequate protection in the form of an express clause. For example, there is an implied term in tort to provide reasonable care and skill in the provision of services, such as when a solicitor provides a professional service to a client. There is also an implied term that goods produced have to be fit for purpose, hence suppliers have to ensure that the goods they supply are fit for the purpose that the consumer is going to use them for.

R v Brown (Criminal)

This is a very explicit case that is particularly infamous amongst law students due to its facts. However, this case also laid down an important principle regarding when someone can consent to harm.

What the case established

The case held that a victim cannot consent to harm in the absence of a good reason – in this case, the satisfying of sado-masochistic desires did not constitute as a 'good reason' for such consent to be valid.

Facts of the case

A group of sado-masochists engaged in consensual acts of violence against each other for sexual gratification and were accordingly charged with various offences under the Offences Against the Person Act 1861 as the victims suffered physical harm as a result of the sexual acts.

What the judge(s) said

The majority of the judges held that it was not in the public interest that a person is allowed to wound or cause actual bodily harm to another for no good reason and, without such a reason, the victim's consent would not be a defence to a charge under the relevant sections of the Offences Against the Person Act 1861. Furthermore, the majority held that the satisfying of sado-masochistic desires did not constitute a good reason. Lastly, since the injuries suffered by the victim were neither transient nor trifling, the victim could not consent to the harm.

Why is this case important

This case sparked immense controversy and the difference in judgment between the majority and minority showed a huge difference in attitude towards whether someone can consent to harmful sexual activity. The majority should disdain towards consenting to harmful sexual activity and held that one will not be allowed to consent to such harm as it would be against the 'public interest'. The minority was less convinced and said that we should not rule out consent for such sexual activity provided that the consent given was valid.

The majority decision was thus the much more conservative decision and academics have argued that the judges should not act as a 'morality police' and disallow individuals from performing certain sexual acts even if both parties are willing and have consented to it. A parallel has been drawn to other 'harmful' activities that can be consented to such as tattooing and body modifications.

The current state of the law

A victim is not allowed to consent to harm that is not 'merely transient and trifling', but this area of law is controversial because it was held in another case that an old married couple was allowed to brandish the husband's initials on the wife's buttocks because it had 'sentimental value' and was not against the public interest (*R v Wilson*). Academics have argued that this shows a moral double standard.

R. (on the application of Miller) v Secretary of State for Exiting the European Union (Constitutional)

Another very recent Supreme Court decision, and possibly the most well-known one due to the immense press coverage it received ever since the Brexit referendum happened.

What the case established

The Supreme Court, perhaps controversially, held that the Government did not have the necessary power under the royal prerogative to give notice pursuant to TEU Art 50(2) for the UK to withdraw from the EU. The Supreme Court held that an Act of Parliament will be required.

Facts of the case

This decision went up to the Supreme Court when Gina Miller challenged the legality of the government giving a formal notice under Art 50 to leave the EU, and this decision raised important constitutional questions regarding the separation of powers between the legislative, executive and judiciary.

What the judge(s) said

The judges reiterated that the European Communities Act 1972 (ECA) formally introduced EU law into English law. It established EU law as a supreme overriding source of domestic law. It was envisaged that any new obligations or rights were only implemented in English law following a variation of the definition of 'Treaties' under the ECA. Hence, the judges held that the Parliament could not have intended that the ECA would continue to bring in new EU law rights if the UK was no longer under the control of EU law. Hence, it was not envisaged that the royal prerogative could bring an end to the UK's legal obligations under EU law. If the UK leaves the EU, they would no longer be bound under EU law – this signifies a major constitutional amendment and the judges stressed that it would be inconsistent with the fundamental principle of parliamentary sovereignty for such a constitutional change to be brought about by the royal prerogative, i.e. executive action alone This is especially so when it was Parliament which decided that EU law should be granted supreme status over English law in the first place.

Hence, the judges concluded that the royal prerogative power exists solely in the international law plane and could not be used to alter a fundamental constitutional right without statutory intervention.

Why is this case important

This case plays a hugely important role in setting out what the constitutional law dictates in an unprecedented situation such as this. It makes it clear that the doctrine of separation of powers should be respected and the executive cannot solely implement a decision that would impinge on the legislative's domain. Since the legislative, i.e. Parliament was the one that introduced the supreme status of EU law into English law in the first place, statutory intervention is needed in order to remove such a status from English law and the royal prerogative alone is not enough to introduce such a fundamental constitutional change.

The current state of the law

Again, this is an unprecedented situation, but this case hopefully sets a precedence for any subsequent events involving the use of the royal prerogative such that the executive, i.e. the government, will not be allowed to exercise their powers to implement a fundamental constitutional amendment in the absence of statutory intervention.

For more example law concepts and cases check *The Ultimate CLT Guide*– flick to the back to get a free copy

WORK EXPERIENCE

Law work experience, whilst not compulsory, can be a good way of indicating an interest in law and showing your initiative and commitment in knowing more about the law by finding out how the law works in practice. Many applicants will have done various shadowing experiences or informal attachments at various law firms, but what makes an applicant truly stand out is the way they reflect on their work experience instead of plainly stating that they have completed a work experience.

Good example of how to describe your work experience:

"I shadowed a criminal barrister during my summer holidays, and it was an eye-opening experience and allowed me to have a better understanding of how criminal law works in practice. I assisted the criminal barrister in preparing a witness statement which will be used in court, and in the process I learnt about how the criminal justice system is heavily dependent on tight procedures governed by the Criminal Procedure Rules. In addition, the adversarial system ensures that a defendant will always be innocent until proven guilty by the prosecution."

Bad example of how to describe your work experience:

"I have completed a week's work experience in a Magic Circle firm and I attended meetings, helped to proofread contracts and mingled with various trainees and associates. This work experience made me interested in becoming a lawyer."

The reason why the first example is better than the second example is because the first candidate made an effort to discuss the legal concepts and rules that he or she has picked up over the work experience, and what they have learnt about the law after the experience. In contrast, the latter candidate merely lists the tasks he or she was made to do during his or her work experience, without linking this back to how it might have made the candidate decide that studying law might be interesting.

Remember – your personal statement should never be a laundry list of your personal achievements or your list of work experience. Whilst you are supposed to put yourself in the best light so as to maximise your chances of receiving an offer, you should always tailor your personal statement such that it shows a genuine interest in studying a subject and makes a tutor believe that you have the academic potential to excel in law, as opposed to coming across as being overly-confident and arrogant.

Many candidates also risk the danger of making their personal statement too saturated with work experience, which makes their personal statement come across as more akin to a job application as opposed to a university application. Remember, law is an **academic** subject at undergraduate level, not a **vocational** subject (at least this is largely true in the UK), and your primary focus should always be to adopt a tone that shows an interest in the academic subject as opposed to the career (in contrast to a subject such a medicine which is more vocational than academic in some universities).

Arranging Work Experience

Arranging work experience can be hard. If you're finding it difficult to get exactly what you want, please don't be disheartened. You are facing the same difficulty that tens of thousands of students before you have also faced.

With work experience, it's a very good idea to start early. The earlier you approach people, the more likely you are to be accepted. It is not really practical to start seeking work experience until after you turn 16 due to age restrictions within the work place – especially where confidential information is concerned! So conduct your work experience during the summer after your GCSE examinations and throughout your AS year. This can be achieved through private arrangements you yourself make but it always worth consulting your schools careers officer as well. Remember that any part-time/summer paid jobs also count as work experience and definitely worth mentioning as they show an additional degree of maturity and professionalism.

If you are able to keep up a small regular commitment over a period of months it really helps to show dedication. It's a good idea to always carry a notebook when you're on work experience. Use it to note down anything interesting you see or hear about to make certain you don't forget!

Types of Work Experience

Law firm attachments
Some law firms run informal attachment programmes aimed at sixth form law students, and these usually have a social mobility slant and are aimed at increasing access to a legal career. These programmes may be good for having a taste as to what commercial lawyers do in practice, and how a law degree might be relevant (for example, learning about contract law and company law and how these subjects might be of interest to you).

Shadowing a barrister
There are many different kinds of barristers, and you can choose to shadow one that specialises in an area of law that might be of interest to you. For example, if you are interested in human rights law, it may be a good idea to get in touch with a chamber that specialises in human rights issues, and this might be a good opportunity for you to find out what human rights law entails. Criminal law barristers are always in need of extra help and are more than willing to accept student volunteers, so this might be a good avenue if you are struggling to find a chamber that has the capacity to take in student volunteers.

Court Visits
Certain cases are open for public viewing, and you do not have to travel all the way done to London just to observe a case – you can simply go to any Magistrates' or Crown Court in your area to observe a case and take some notes as to how barristers argue their case in front of the judge in order to defend their client, or how a prosecutor presents a case in order to determine a defendant's guilt.

Volunteering
Volunteering in your local community is also an excellent way of demonstrating an interest in law and finding out more about how law works in practice. For example, volunteering in a free legal advice clinic can be a good way of observing how lawyers engage in pro bono work and provide free legal advice for defendants who are not able to afford a lawyer. Your role might be limited to administrative work as you are not a legally-qualified lawyer, but you should give it your all in any tasks that are assigned to you and you will be surprised how much you can learn even by doing simple tasks.

Attending Courses
There are plenty of introductory law courses designed to provide students with a basic understanding of the law and help them decide whether studying law is something that they are suited for – for example universities typically run such courses designed to attract sixth form law students to apply to their universities and also increase access to the subject.

Extra-Curricular

Extra-curricular activities that are related to law are a good way of indicating your interest in law and your initiative in finding out more about an unfamiliar subject. However, many students fall into the trap of merely listing out their extra-curricular activities, be it being in a sports team or playing a musical instrument without actively trying to make this relevant to why they want to study law in the first place. Whilst your extra-curricular activity does not strictly have to be related to law, students who are able to forge a connection between their extra-curricular activity and the study of law will stand out in the crowd and improve their chances of receiving an offer.

A good example of talking about your extra-curricular activity

"I was the secretary of my tennis club and I would regularly attend meetings with teachers and students in order to discuss about our club activities. As the secretary, I was able to cultivate and improve my thinking and writing skills, as I was regularly tasked to write up and present several proposals to the teachers for approval. I believe such skills will benefit me in the studying of law as I will be able to assimilate information from numerous written sources and come up with my own critical opinion."

A bad example of talking about your extra-curricular activity

"As the captain of my sixth form's rowing team, I displayed exceptional leadership skills and resilience. Not only did I have to commit to training six times a week for our competitions, I also had to steer the team towards a common goal and ensure that everyone was motivated and kept on top of their fitness."

The first example shows an effort to draw a link between the student's extra-curricular activity and how this is relevant to studying law, whilst the second example did not make a similar effort. The second example also comes across as merely boasting about one's achievement, without actually showing how being the captain of a rowing team might exhibit certain skills and attributes that are relevant for a good law student.

There are many different extra-curricular activities that can be relevant to the study of law, here are a few non-exhaustive suggestions:

➢ Community work
➢ Sports
➢ Book clubs
➢ Student law societies
➢ Debating
➢ Music
➢ Art

What tutors look out for in a good law student

Above all, it is necessary to display certain qualities in your personal statement that will make an admission tutor confident that you are well-suited for the study of law and you are likely to excel in the course. The tutors are not looking out for good lawyers – a good law student does not always equate to a good lawyer, and vice versa! Here are a few factors that might indicate that a candidate is possibly going to be a good potential law student:

Ability to think critically

It is absolutely crucial that law students know how to think critically and analyse complex issues based on their readings. The law is complex and an undergraduate law course tends to deal with novel situations that are always not as clear-cut and require a high level of critical analysis. The law is also always in a constant state of flux and law students are always expected to debate and analyse whether the law is satisfactory as it is or should be subject to changes.

Examples of how you can show the ability to think critically is to discuss certain topics that might be of interest to you in your personal statement, and what your opinion is based on the information that is available to you. This might be picked up on further in the interview, if there is one. A good analysis of a topic, such as in politics, law or philosophy, is always an excellent indicator that a student is able to think critically and form an informed opinion about difficult issues.

A strong command of the English language

Law students cannot shy away from copious amounts of readings – students on average have to study five different law subjects in a year, and each subject can demand up to a few hundred pages of readings in a week during term time – law is not for the faint-hearted! Without a strong command of the English language, tutors will not be convinced that you will be able to handle the large amounts of readings and be able to write effective, coherent essays. Unlike other subjects such as English or Literature, law does not expect flamboyant language or superfluous vocabulary – on the contrary, law students are expected to write in simple, plain English that is effective and to the point. You will want to make sure that your personal statement reflects this – avoid unnecessary filler words, avoid overly-complex vocabulary if a simpler word may convey a meaning more effectively, and ensure that your grammar and spelling is as flawless as possible.

Academic curiosity

Law students are not expected to just memorise heaps of statutes and cases and regurgitate them during examinations, contrary to popular belief. If that was the case, we can simply get machines to act as lawyers! Admission tutors want to see that a student is curious about the law and has the initiative to find out more about the law and engage in further reading and research in order to fully explore a topic of interest. Law is a subject that emphasises heavily on independent self-learning, in contrast to the science subjects where they may be more contact hours. Hence, a lack of self-discipline indicates that a student will not likely excel in a law degree, and tutors want to make sure that a student is genuinely interested in the law and has the self-discipline and drive to do well in their undergraduate course. Therefore, a student should show a certain level of academic curiosity, whether by discussing about certain readings that have sparked an interest in the student, or reading up about certain legal issues happening in the real world.

Intelligence

Sometimes, academic grades alone are insufficient to accurately gauge a student's intelligence. Many students only happen to achieve good grades through route-learning, or by their teachers constantly pushing them and spoon-feeding them with instructions on how to do well for standardised examinations. Admission tutors want to admit the brightest students into law school, as it is an academically-rigorous course and bright students tend to do well in the law course. On top of achieving good grades, admission tutors want to see that a student has the intellect-level necessary to do well in law, and you should seek to show this by not being afraid to have a thorough discussion about topics of interest in your personal statement and showing that you are capable of understanding complex issues and dissecting certain topics.

Time-management

As mentioned earlier, law is a subject that emphasises on independent self-learning and admission tutors want to be confident that a student is able to manage his or her time well during the law course. There are plenty of ways to indicate good time-management, such as talking about how you manage to do plenty of further reading or extra-curricular activities on top of keeping up with your studies.

Awareness of moral and ethical issues

Law is an area that is deeply entwined with moral and ethical issues. When students discuss about certain legal or political issues, it is always imperative for them to spot certain moral and ethical issues that might arise, and how might they be resolved. These issues tend to form a grey area and students can take this opportunity to show that they have the intellectual capacity and ability to critically think about what is right and what is wrong.

Motivation

A student who comes across as highly-motivated and clear about why they want to study law in their personal statement will stand a much better chance of securing an offer. Some students make the mistake of coming across as muddled or unsure in their personal statement, such as giving generic reasons why they want to study law. For example, simply stating that law is 'interesting' or 'stimulating' alone will not make a candidate stand out – more explanation is needed in order to convince an admission tutor that you are truly motivated and clear about why you want to study law. As usual, avoid certain clichés if possible such as 'wanting to save the world' or wanting to 'be a champion of human rights' – such reasons tend to come across as disingenuous, unless a candidate has a strong back-story and personal reason to support such a grandiose claim.

Subject choice

Many candidates have the misperception that in order to study law, they should stick to essay-based subjects for their A levels or IB examinations such as History, Literature or Geography – this is not true at all. Even though law is generally classified as an arts subject, it requires a lot of problem-solving skills and examinations can come in the form of argumentative essay-type questions or problem questions whereby you are asked to solve a client's legal problems. Science students are also favoured due to their ability to solve problems and their ability to show logical thinking, and many law students do have a science background. You should not choose a subject based on the fact that it might be more 'relevant' to law (e.g. some tutors actually discourage students from taking law at A levels), you should always choose subjects that you are confident you will score well in so as to increase your chances of meeting the minimum grade requirements.

Achievements and awards

Lastly, winning book prizes or debating competitions are always good indicators of a potential good law student, as such achievements and awards show a student's ability to write and communicate effectively. Of course, many students are able to secure spots in top law schools without necessarily winning any awards, and such awards will not make up for a bad personal statement or bad grades.

OXBRIDGE

The main difference between Oxbridge and the other law schools will be the fact that you generally cannot secure a place in Oxbridge without doing an admission test and an **interview**. In fact, Oxford and Cambridge are the only law schools in the UK to conduct interviews – most other law schools might only have an admission test at most.

There is a common perception that the Oxford law course tends to be more theoretical than Cambridge (Oxford calls their law degree 'jurisprudence', which is the philosophy of law), whereas Cambridge has a focus on 'black-letter law' (e.g. company law, commercial law). Such perceptions are generally stereotypical in nature and should not affect your choice of either university to a large extent, in fact most candidates can hardly differentiate the difference.

Here are some subtle differences between Oxford and Cambridge if this is of importance to you:

OXFORD	CAMBRIDGE
Students only have two sets of examinations – preliminary examinations during the second term of their first year, and final examinations (9 papers spread over two weeks which can be very demanding), only the final year examinations count towards your overall grades	Cambridge has the Tripos system – students essentially do a final exam at the end of the year (4 to 5 papers), but do not receive an overall grade (each year is counted separately)
Jurisprudence is compulsory	Jurisprudence is not compulsory but can be done as a subject in second or third year
Generally students get less optional modules to choose from (only two optional modules on top of the seven core modules)	Generally more optional modules to choose from (seven optional modules on top of the seven core modules)
Has a reputation for being more theoretical	Has a reputation for being more 'black-letter'
Uses the LNAT	Uses the Cambridge Law Test
Does not use the SAQ	Uses the SAQ
Shortlists less applicants for interview (about 40%)	Shortlists more applicants for interview (about 80%)
Pools applicants before the interview	Pools applicants after the interview

One important thing to take note of is the fact that **the Oxbridge deadline is earlier** – 15th October for your UCAS submission. Hence, Oxbridge applicants tend to have to prepare their application earlier and be prepared to take the LNAT or Cambridge Law Test as well as to attend the interview if they are shortlisted. Some colleges may also request for marked written work, which is usually essays you have done in class that have been marked by your teachers.

Cambridge also has an additional section called the Supplementary Answer Questionnaire (SAQ) which is to allow students to explain why they want to apply to Cambridge in particular (as your personal statement will tend to be more generic as it is sent out to five different universities). Oxford does not have a similar system.

DEFERRED ENTRY & GAP YEARS

It is always advisable to apply to university during your A2 year – at the very least it is a useful experience and you can always apply again next year if you are unsuccessful. In attending university a year later, you are a year older, bringing more maturity and life experience to the course – the benefits of this are clear to see in course like law!

If you are planning to take a gap year, always apply whilst in A-level year unless there is a reason you would not be able to gain a place (e.g. grades/predictions too low, you need to sit more exams). Applying for deferred entry allows you to go on your gap year, safe in the knowledge that you have secured a place upon your return. If things then don't go to plan, you have time to improve your application and a second chance in which to apply to different law schools.

You'll need to tweak your statement slightly if you're applying for deferred entry. You will need to demonstrate to the tutor that you are filling your gap year with meaningful experiences in order to help you grow as a person. Therefore discuss your gap year plans in a brief paragraph, describing what you hope to achieve, what life skills you hope to learn, and how these are both transferable and applicable to your course. In addition, a year of deferred entry gives you opportunity to work and save in order to fund your progress through what is a very expensive time at university.

This is a good opportunity once again to show your commitment. If your gap year plans include any volunteering work, use this to support your vocation of public service. If you have already made plans, it shows that you're organised.

To make a strong application, you should be spending a significant proportion of your gap year doing things that support your application: work experience, voluntary work and activities that build your skills. Discuss in your personal statement why you chose to do these things, what you are learning from them and how it has affected your desire to study law. Make sure you account for all time and give reasons for everything you do, tying it back to your path towards studying law. A good application should draw upon your gap year to reinforce your skills and commitment; it should give positive reasons why you have chosen to take a gap year. Taking a gap year gives you good opportunities to expand your experiences, but you have to remember that it also brings expectations – therefore if you don't take these opportunities you stand to weaken your application.

Going on a gap year is a choice for you to make; overall, you are equally likely to get an offer with or without taking a gap year.

Re-applying

If instead you are reading this during a gap year because of an unsuccessful first application do not be disheartened. Applying a second time puts you in a much stronger position as you have your A-level grades in hand. Do mention your failure first time round in your personal statement, but also reflect on it and discuss why you think this happened. More importantly, discuss what you have done to address these issues to improve yourself as a candidate. Re-applying shows strength of character, resilience and determination- qualities desired by any course tutor at any institution.

MATURE & GRADUATE APPLICANTS

If you're applying as a mature student or to graduate entry law, talking about your previous work and career is important.

If you have been working for a number of years, then a large chunk of your relevant life story will be due to your employment. Your journey to law will describe your previous career path, the moment you thought about a change, how you investigated the study of law and why you now believe it is the right path for you.

Coming from a professional background, the skills you have learned in the workplace will be significant and begin to overtake extra-curricular activities as a way of demonstrating core attributes such as time-management, communication and team working. In addition, you may have undertaken professional learning in your job such as reading books or attending courses – be sure to draw upon this to support your ability to undertake the rigorous learning required of a law student.

Admissions tutors are not looking to see how similar your current job is to law. You will learn what you need to know at law school. They are looking for the general skills you have learned that will help make you a good law student, and research/experience outside of work to confirm your interest.

Standing out from the crowd

You may have heard people saying that a good personal statement helps you stand out from the crowd – and this is certainly true. Admissions tutors read hundreds of personal statements, so to be in with the best chance yours should offer something a bit different to leave a lasting good impression.

Whilst standing out from the crowd is easy, the line between standing out for the right and the wrong reasons is a fine one and you have to tread carefully.

The easiest ways to add some originality are in your reading and activities. There will be countless people who play football but less who play ice hockey; everyone has read Letters to a Law Student, but fewer may have read books that are less well-known. It is not more valuable to do something less popular, but it can make it easier for the reader to see your personal statement as original. This is not about going out and enrolling with an extreme ironing club – it is about taking time to identify the things you already do and skills you have that are a bit more interesting than the generic activities and just giving them a mention to show a wide variety of interests.

Many law schools will score the personal statement based on a marking grid. You'll gain marks for evidence of performance in different areas depending on your assessed level of achievement. These areas may include interest in law, variety of work experience, evidence of further reading, critical thinking skills and English language ability. Ensure you cover all the areas described in the section guide to make sure you hit all the key scoring points.

Proof-reading the personal statement is extremely important – not just you, but also by showing it to friends, family and teachers to get their opinions. Firstly, it's so easy to ignore your own mistakes, because as you become familiar with your own work you begin skimming through rather than reading in-depth. But also, this allows people to assess the writing style – by gathering lots of opinions you can build up a good idea of the strongest areas (which you should expand) and the weakest areas (which you should modify).

Don't try to force anything into the personal statement. Allow it to grow and showcase your wide variety of skills. Make sure there is a smooth flow from one idea to the next. Allow it to tell your story. Make sure all the spelling and grammar are accurate. Then, your personal statement will shine out from the average ones to give you the best possible chance.

Omissions

It can be difficult to work out exactly where the line stands when it comes to omitting certain information - sometimes leaving certain things out can cause problems.

For example, let's imagine you worked for half an hour a month at a legal clinic for over a 6 month period. If you said in your personal statement you had worked at a legal clinic for 6 months, you could reasonably expect interview questions on it. If it emerged that you had only spent three hours there in total, the interviewer would be left doubting the truthfulness of the whole personal statement.

Another circumstance when not to omit details is when there is something that needs explaining. Perhaps you've taken a year out of the normal education pathway to do something different or because you were experiencing some difficulty. Whilst the personal statement is not the place to discuss extenuating circumstances, it should tell the story of your recent path through life. If there are any big gaps, it is likely to concern the person reading it that you have something to hide. Make sure you explain your route and the reasons for it, putting it in the context of your journey towards being a law student.

Interviews

As mentioned above, Oxford and Cambridge tend to be the only universities that will interview for law. The interview has a very high weightage in determining whether a student receives an offer, and a student with a bad interview score will very rarely receive an offer.

Interviews tend to be graded from a scale of 1-10, with 1 being definitely not worthy of an offer and 10 being definitely worthy of an offer. Successful candidates tend to score at least a 7 on the interview.

The types of interview that you can expect will vary between different colleges, but they can be generally split into two different types of interview.

General interview

A general interview will tend to focus on your personal statement and talk about why you are interested in studying law, what you have been doing in school so far and why you decided to apply to a particular college. These interviews tend to be more straightforward, but you should always know your personal statement inside out and be prepared to defend anything you have mentioned in your personal statement – this is why you should definitely not exaggerate or make up facts in your personal statement, especially when they might be picked up on during the interviews!

Technical interview

This is where the tutors will be keen on observing whether you are able to think like a law student. For example, they might give you an article to read beforehand, and ask you certain challenging questions based on the article in order to probe you and see you how respond under pressure and think on your feet. Some tutors might simply talk about anything that is of interest to them and see how you respond to certain questions. This interview may be hard to prepare for due to its unpredictability, but it is generally expected of students to do thorough research beforehand and read up as widely as possible in order to have a wealth of information they can draw from.

Things to Avoid

Whilst there are no rights and wrongs to writing a personal statement, there are a few common traps students can easily fall into. Here follows a discussion of things that are best avoided to ensure your personal statement is strong.

Stating the obvious – this includes phrases like "I am studying A-level history which has helped me learn about World War II". Admissions tutors can see from the UCAS form what A-level subjects you are studying and the learning you claim is obvious.

University names – the same personal statement goes to all universities, so don't include any university names. Only include specifics of the course if they are common to all the courses you are applying to.

Controversy – avoid controversy in any form, be it strong opinions or any other reason. You don't want to make an impression for the wrong reasons, and if you irritate the reader you're making life needlessly difficult.

Lists – everything needs to be included for a reason. Very few things have an intrinsic value, rather the value comes from the knowledge you gain and the skills you develop by doing the activities. Therefore, reeling off a long list of sports you play won't impress anyone. Instead, focus on specifics and indicate what you have learned from doing each thing you mention.

Detail about your A-level subjects – most law applicants study similar A-levels and they are included on your UCAS form. This won't help you stand out and is a waste of words.

Things that happened before GCSE – if something *started* when you were nine and you have continued it up until today then you should absolutely include it as it shows great commitment and the opportunity to develop many skills. However, if you are considering mentioning the archery you stopped four years ago, please resist the temptation. Putting something that finished a long time ago signals to the reader that you don't have much going on now – not the impression you want to be making.

Include books you haven't read – this is risky. Even if you *genuinely* intend to read the book, you can't make any intelligent observations about it if you haven't done so yet. In addition, you are then committed to finishing it even if you find it very dull, or you risk being caught out in an interview. Stick to things you have already read. If you don't have much to say, pick some short books and journal articles and make a start today!

Extenuating circumstances – the personal statement is to tell your story. It is not the place for extenuating circumstances. If any are applicable, this is for teachers to write in the reference. Make sure you know who is writing it and meet with them to help explain the full story.

Plagiarism – it goes without saying that you must not plagiarise, but I feel no "things to avoid" list would be complete without the most important point. Plagiarism of another personal statement is the easiest way to get yourself into big trouble. UCAS use sophisticated detection software and if any significant match shows up (not necessarily the whole statement, just a few identical sentences is enough), then universities you apply to will be notified and are likely to blacklist your application.

The Reference

The UCAS reference is often neglected by many applicants; it's an untapped resource that can give you an edge over other applicants. In order to plan your use of the reference you first need to establish how it will be used – again consult prospectuses or subject websites. Does it actually count towards your application score or rather is it only consulted in border line candidates? Furthermore the reference could certainly affect the way in which the tutor perceives what you have written and indeed what they infer from it.

Either way, in order to get the most out of your reference you need to actively participate in its creation. The best way to achieve this is to ask a teacher who you are particularly friendly with to write it. Even if this is not possible, ask for a copy of your reference before it is submitted to UCAS. This way you can ensure that the personal statement and reference complement one another for maximum impact.

The reference is best used for explanations of negative aspects within your application – e.g. deflated exam results, family bereavements – or even addition of new information if you run out of space in your personal statement. In this respect the reference is a backdoor through which you can feed more information to the tutor in order to strengthen your application.

If there is a teacher who is willing to go through your reference with you, complete your personal statement first before starting on the reference itself. This way you will have a clear idea of the content and tone of the majority of your application as well as anything that may be missing which you would like to add.

The reference is the one place for your teachers to be completely unreserved - superlatives and complements mean a lot more coming from someone other than yourself. One such example of this is the opportunity for your teachers to discuss how they have actively noticed your initiative and passion, going above and beyond in pursuing the subject in question.

EXAMPLE PERSONAL STATEMENTS

Below you will find five example personal statements of successful law applicants, with comments drawing your attention to the stronger and weaker points of that personal statement.

To make best use, don't look immediately at this. First, read the personal statement yourself and get a feeling for the general style of writing. Then, test yourself: decide which you think the strongest and weakest parts are. After that, look at the comments on the statement. By using the book this way, you develop your own critical reading skills – skills which you can then apply to your own personal statement, allowing you to build in improvements.

> IT CANNOT BE OVERSTRESSED HOW IMPORTANT IT IS THAT YOU **DO NOT COPY** FROM THESE PERSONAL STATEMENTS

Rather use them for inspiration. Plagiarism is a breach of academic responsibility and is highly likely to be detected by UCAS's *Copycatch* software.

Personal Statement 1

My academic and personal experience of law has led me to believe that it is an integral and vibrant field of study. Indeed, law is intertwined with, and embraces every aspect of our lives on Earth, extending to the very composition, occupation and history of the planet. My A level subjects have confirmed this idea for me. From History, I have seen the terrible consequences of one man taking the law into his own hands, as Hitler did through the Enabling Act (1933). In Geography, I have been angered by the injustice of trade laws, and the way they continue to hamper development in the world's least developed countries. One of the reasons I have chosen to study French is my hope that it will create possibilities to practice as a lawyer in other jurisdictions, particularly French speaking African nations.

I am most interested in International Law and because of this I have chosen to undertake an Extended Project Qualification on the subject of the legality of the Nuremburg Trials and the legal precedent they set. I also aim to incorporate research into the International Criminal Court, and how the trials led to its establishment.

To further my understanding of Law, I organised and undertook a week of work experience at Albion Chambers, Bristol in July 2010. Working with highly skilled barristers was incredibly exciting, as was the opportunity to examine CCTV evidence and sit in on interviews with clients. It was a poignant experience, as I saw how our justice system can acquit those wrongly accused, while also protecting society.

I have read a number of enlightening books such as 'The Law Machine' by Marcel Berlins and Claire Dyer and 'Invitation to Law' by A. W. B. Simpson, and have gained a greater understanding of legal basics such as the criminal process and the law of torts. Reading the book 'Eve was Framed' by Helena Kennedy has also been fascinating, as I have started to think about issues which I had never before considered – how Law might be affected by gender. Since watching two documentaries about jails in Miami, Florida, I have also become interested in the differences between the British and American legal systems.

In addition to broadening my knowledge of our legal system, I have sought to develop skills which I believe will assist me in studying and practising law. As an active member of my Sixth Form's Debating Society, I have gained the ability to analyse an argument, and also developed my confidence in terms of public speaking. Later this year, I intend to speak at a Mock United Nations Summit, in which I will help to represent one country and their interests. This has developed both my confidence in public speaking and my ability to analyse and construct arguments. During the last year, I have been undertaking a Duke of Edinburgh Gold Award at Sixth Form. This has developed the necessary organisational skills for a high pressure law degree. In fact, I have already completed one of the sections, and am well on my way to completing two more.

For the past year, I have been giving up two free lessons per fortnight to assist in a Year 11 Maths class, helping students on the C/ D grade borderline. I have learned how to explain complex concepts to pupils who struggle to understand: I believe this will aid me greatly if I achieve my ambition of becoming a barrister.

Furthermore, I am a leader of a Sunday school group at my church, where I often organise games and activities for the children. This has helped to develop my interpersonal skills crucial for practising as a Lawyer. I also attend a drama class each week at Bristol Old Vic and play for my Sixth Form's netball team.

My studies, work experience and research thus far have shown me that law presents no intellectual boundaries; it is real and relevant, continuous and alive. I am excited by the prospect of studying law and relish the opportunity to study such a dynamic subject at university.

Universities applied to:
➢ Oxford: Offer
➢ Durham: Offer
➢ Nottingham: Offer
➢ Cardiff: Offer
➢ Reading: Offer

Good Points:
This personal statement is very well-written and well-structured with very few grammatical errors or omissions. It clearly demonstrates that the student has made a conscious effort to engage with aspects of the subject they wish to study at university; both within their current academic study (making direct reference to their A level subjects) and in terms of their extra-curricular activities. This wide range of activities and experiences are all made to seem relevant to law and act as evidence that the course chosen is one the student has carefully considered and will enjoy. The closing two lines are particularly strong, acting as a punchy reiteration of why the student wants to study law.

Bad Points:
When talking about the wider reading or extra-curricular activities that they have undertaken, the student could have taken the statement one step further by making explicit reference to why each was chosen or what they particularly enjoyed or learned. Moreover, several references were made to the student's desire to work as a barrister and pursue a career in law. While it is good to show such ambition, it should be remembered that applicants are applying to academic institutions to study, and universities will appreciate that the student is looking forward to studying law as an academic discipline rather than a means to an end vocation.

Overall:
This is a strong personal statement overall which was clearly well-received. However, it would have benefitted from the student talking in greater depth about what they learned or enjoyed in particular when completing extra-curricular activities or wider reading. The student needed to do more than say that the activity is relevant to law; they needed to go on to explain why they thought this. Specific examples would have helped. The wider engagement with the subject is to be commended, however, being especially necessary, the subject being applied for is not one which the student currently studies in school.

Personal Statement 2

I view the practice of law as an analytical debate that sees lawyers and judges treading between theoretical law and the chaotic reality of society to clarify the scope of what is right. It is this mental challenge that inspired me to a career as a public attorney with the goal of joining the judiciary.

My interest was kindled when I first undertook my IB History Extended Essay. I enjoyed developing persuasive arguments, taking into account History's investigative and systematic nature. This was a unique challenge since my topic was in an entrenched area of study and involved formulating a strong original thesis that could stand against established historians. My efforts were validated when my essay was selected for publication in the June 2013 issue of the renowned academic journal, The Concord Review. Such an adversarial mental struggle strongly appealed to me and sparked my enthusiasm for a legal career that would allow me to tackle such challenges daily.

I pursued my interest by interning at Rajah & Tann (under the Junior College Law Programme), Drew & Napier and Kim & Co, some of the most competitive and prestigious law firms in Singapore. I learnt an extensive range of practical legal skills as I drafted affidavits, submissions, researched case law and created opinions on points of law. As I became familiar with family and civil litigation law, I learned how to devise compelling arguments by contextualizing vague laws to complex situations. Once, I was involved in a correspondence with the Attorney General Chambers (AGC) appealing a charge of overstaying. This entailed researching immigration laws relevant to our client's unique circumstance. While the arresting officer was sceptical of having the charges overturned, we successfully convinced the AGC otherwise. Such experiences have given me varied perspectives of the legal world, not only of theoretical concepts but also of the practical procedures that are built upon them, laying the foundation for my foray into the legal world.

I have also kept myself updated of legal developments, notably when Singapore relaxed legislative requirements of what constitutes an arbitration agreement. I could relate to this as I took part in a noted case that involved the term 'mediation' in an arbitration clause. It was intriguing framing arguments differentiating mediation with arbitration. Through my practical experiences, I have been stimulated to critically consider the effect of dynamic legislation on legal cases. I was also fascinated by the lecture series 'Justice' by Harvard law professor Michael Sandel, in which he applies moral perspectives to perennial issues such as proportional retribution in the context of historical injustices.

I have taken the initiative of founding a start-up, 'MobForest', consisting of a team of 7 that hosts project challenges for students to tackle in return for prizes. As part of MobForest, I helped to draft contracts with companies sponsoring the challenges. I also read up on Singapore's legal environment to determine our business obligations as well as on Intellectual Property rights as a means to protect our platform. Forming MobForest gave me valuable insight into the practical legal demands of a business as well as the confidence to approach clients.

Simultaneously, my National Service duty as a Sergeant and subsequently as a Lieutenant of Singapore's fire fighting force (SCDF) saw me leading a platoon of men in fire and rescue incidents. As a platoon commander, one of the obstacles to executing a task is the poor phrasing of orders. Given the chaotic nature of a fire incident, it is important that commands given successfully convey the task at hand, with each man clear of their role.

Universities applied to:
➢ Cambridge: Interview + Rejected
➢ London School of Economics: Offer
➢ University College London: Offer
➢ King's: Offer
➢ Nottingham: Offer

Good Points:

The personal statement is well-written, showing a clear and logical structure and having no grammatical errors. The student shows a clear commitment to law by having an impressive array of extra-curricular activities, which act as evidence of their genuine interest in the legal world. It is clear that the student follows current legal affairs and takes any opportunity they get to engage with law. The reference to the lecture by Sandel is a particularly strong inclusion to this effect as it is clearly an academic mode of engaging with legal study and academic debate.

Bad Points:

While the student has a wealth of legal experience, the focus is very much on law in a business or commercial setting. It should be remembered when applying to study subjects with clear career routes (such as law) that a university will be looking for a genuine interest in studying law as an academic discipline rather than as a means of securing a job. After all, a law degree is not a pre-requisite for a legal career; a law degree is not necessary to take the GDL or LPC, for example. Additionally, the student's more relevant activities to university study, such as the extended essay or the lecture, are given minimal attention and explanation, when in reality they would be the most beneficial aspects to emphasise.

Overall:

This is a strong personal statement but struggles with the placement of emphasis. While business and vocational activities show a strong commitment to law, their weighting in this personal statement is at the expense of more traditionally academic interests. It is these latter interests and modes of engaging with legal theory that would better impress a university. The student could undertake some wider reading in a legal area they know they will be studying should they secure a place on the course that genuinely interests them (such as one of the seven foundation subjects in law). With this, they should include more examples of textbooks, articles or legal papers in this area to emphasise their research interests.

Personal Statement 3

Law is the epitome of human reason; it is the force that holds society together and the cornerstone on which great civilizations were built upon. By dictating a code of conduct which everyone had to abide by, it has created a system of accountability and allowed society to flourish. However, Law is never static. It changes with time - internalising new concepts and discarding anachronistic ones to reflect societal norms. It is this dynamic nature of the Law that I find so enthralling - that there exists a gamut of good answers but never a right one. Such idealism aside, I believe excellence in legal study and work does not come easy. It requires much passion, intellect and hard work.

At College, I offered 12 academic units (as compared to the standard 10 academic units) at the Singapore-Cambridge GCE 'A' Level Examinations. Concurrently, I represented Singapore in Swimming and was an active member of my College's Swimming and Cross-Country team, training up to six times each week and achieving numerous medals and accolades in Inter-College Competitions. Such excellence in both sports and academics demonstrates my strong self-discipline, time management skills as well as my capacity for sustained hard work.

As a student, I held numerous leadership positions such as Swimming Captain, School Prefect as well as being part of the Executive Committee of my College Freshman Orientation Camp. In addition, I undertook various community-based service projects aimed at spreading awareness on and assuaging the plight of the less-privileged in society. These experiences in positions of influence and leadership have strengthened my organisational and problem solving skills, teamwork as well as allowed me to develop effective communication skills.

For my ability to balance studies, sports and leadership roles, I was among the ten students (out of nine hundred) on my College's prestigious Principal's Honour Roll in 2011 that acknowledged distinguished academic achievement and outstanding contributions to the College. Though challenging as it might have been, I have benefited greatly from my overall College experience and would certainly look forward to continue to represent, contribute and excel in University.

During my National Service stint, I served as a Military Officer entrusted with the responsibility of leading and nurturing the next generation of soldiers. Besides leading soldiers out in the field, I had to handle soldiers from a myriad of backgrounds as well as run the general day to day administration of the battalion. I have had multiple opportunities to serve as a Defending Officer to servicemen (who were accused of various wrongdoings) in military courts as well as conduct investigations into various malpractices in my battalion. These unique and far-reaching dealings in the Army has reaffirmed my decision to pursue law, refined my ability to think critically and to work under significant constraints and duress.

I am a firm believer in the importance of reading and see it as an avenue for the pursuit of knowledge. I read on a wide range of topics including legal conundrums, science, philosophy and even military tactics as I believe sufficient breath of thought is needed to develop one's mental prowess. Through such extensive reading, I have honed my rigour of thought and widened my perspectives to a myriad of issues.

A career in law is diverse and dynamic, yet fraught with many challenges. Legal theory, evidence, clientele management and not to mention regularly navigating the bureaucratic quagmire; no other field is as challenging or multi-faceted as the field of law. Though arduous, I relish the intellectual challenges of legal study and aspire to ensure human rationale and justice continues to prevail in society. Thus, I believe I possess the necessary attributes needed for legal study and excellence in the field of law.

Universities applied to:
- Cambridge: Offer
- London School of Economics: Rejected
- University College London: Rejected

Good Points:
The personal statement is well-written with no obvious errors. The student opens with quite a conceptual statement of what law means to them and this helps to make the subject seem like a well-thought-through choice. Additionally, the student recognises that law is a difficult and challenging course but seems unafraid of the need to put the necessary effort into it. The conclusion is similar in this respect, tying back to the introductory thoughts and ending on a strong statement of why the student feels like they would be a strong candidate to study law at university. Moreover, the student gives a very capable impression by mentioning their place on the College's Honour Roll, as it suggests they can balance their extra-curricular activities with (and not to the detriment of) their academic studies well.

Bad Points:
Structurally, this statement needs to be reorganised. The student's legal interests are given attention and evidence far too late with extra-curricular activities of limited relevance being introduced closer to the beginning. In a personal statement as part of a law application, law needs to be the primary focus throughout. The student's positions of responsibility also come above their academic, legal interests, when they should be given less focus and come later on in the statement. When talking about the skills they developed in relation to these activities, the student makes these developed attributes sound beneficial but does not explicitly tie them to law or why they are useful to the study of law. It takes until the penultimate paragraph for the student to talk openly about their academic interests, and even then, they do not illustrate this with any specific legal examples.

Overall:
The personal statement is good but could be easily improved. The student would benefit from reordering the structure of the content to open with legal or academic interests, and then saving less relevant extra-curricular activities till the end. Any activity or skill should be tied back to law wherever possible – giving specific examples of how they relate would also be helpful in getting across why the student is prepared to study law at university.

Personal Statement 4

Law is a set of rules and guidelines imposed upon a society which reflect its moral consciousness, guided and guarded by the judiciary. I believe everyone has the right to be judged objectively by their own laws. I am fascinated by the process of examining legal arguments, by how the outcome of a case hinges on presentation of the evidence and by the law's status as the ultimate arbiter of 'justice.' It is this desire to study the analytical process and underlying principles of jurisprudence that motivates me to study law academically.

Preparing for my extended project, I studied Plato's Republic and how his analyses of different societies are relevant to modern Britain. Examining the common flaws between our own society and those depicted in Republic made me appreciate the subtlety of the law in its present-day form: many of Plato's proposed solutions to these flaws undermined what are viewed today as personal rights. This led me to reflect on how laws protect us, and also how their intricacies create a doctrine to which people adhere, both complying and incorporating it in their own morality.

Investigating Plato's ideal political system, I considered the contrast between how his laws were devised and their status in our own society. Plato's 'Guardians' (not unlike our own judiciary) were relied on both to codify and interpret the law. While their decisions were considered to be benevolent, society was expected to conform to laws dictated by a separate class. The situation in the UK is quite different: statute law, as well as case law, often reflects current popular opinion. Sarah's law (the parents' right to check the criminal record of any carer for their child) was the direct result of a popular campaign. Whether it is better to have a system of laws that evolve with society or one that is dictated by a separate body is just one example of the ethical questions behind the law that intrigue me.

Seeking experience in the area of law that first attracted me, I assisted a criminal barrister in a Bristol chambers, including client interviews for petty offences and note taking in Crown Court, where we were prosecuting an alleged serial attempted rapist. The defendant's decision to dismiss his lawyers to defend himself brought home the need for a professional intermediary to ensure fair interaction of the individual with the protocol of the law. Examining case files while shadowing a Queen's Counsel specialising in public and taxation law, I was struck by how even the most powerful individual or company is still bound to observe the law. I sought exposure to corporate and commercial law with a local solicitor, where I worked through a practical example of employment law to determine whether a client had a case. This close reading of legal documents was a rewarding and stimulating experience, confirming my commitment to study law.

Captaining rugby teams at school (now 1st XV), club and county level, I have learned how to listen and how to lead; understanding and incorporating others' opinions or feelings in my interaction was key to encouraging progress for the individual or group, to motivate them and help them achieve their own potential. I developed these skills further mentoring in French and as a Sports Ambassador for local primary schools.

Rugby is like society: there are fixed laws that define the game and how it is played, but they are constantly tested by the flair of the players. As a result, the referee must both interpret and enforce the application of those laws; in Plato's terms, he is both guardian and auxiliary. The application of the law to dynamic situations and how different outcomes might be achieved depending upon points of interpretation has fascinated me for years.

I am strongly motivated to study the law's mechanics and with this passion, combined with the necessary determination and underlying skills, I will relish the task of appreciating and mastering law as an intellectual discipline in its own right.

Universities applied to:
➢ Oxford: Offer
➢ University College London: Offer
➢ King's: Offer
➢ Bristol: Offer
➢ Exeter: Offer

Good Points:

This is an impressive personal statement in many regards and was clearly well-received. The student opens with a definition of law but then goes on to interpret what they understand it to mean, and by doing so, has given some insight into their personality and understanding. It is clear from the outset that the student's interest is an academic one, and this will gain them favour from top academic institutions if sustained. The discussion of the student's extended project is given a clear legal dimension and the student competently makes cross-links, which display their strong grasp of sources of UK law - having a current example to underline this point. In this instance, the discussion of work experience complements the academic interests well because of the way the statement is structured – by saving work experience till later, the student made clear that their primary focus is academic and intellectual, but they do have a commitment to engaging with the subject at a practical level.

Bad Points:

Having two paragraphs about rugby probably gives the sport more attention than is necessary. Moreover, while the student has endeavoured to present all their skills as relevant to law, the links can read as somewhat tenuous, particularly in the sporting examples. Replacing one of these paragraphs with one about some wider reading in a purely legal area of interest (as opposed to reading as part of the extended project) would have been a more beneficial addition.

Overall:

This is an extremely strong personal statement. The student clearly gets across their interest in studying law, but more than this, it is unquestionable that their interest is in studying law as an academic discipline rather than practicing law as a career once they have graduated. Structurally, the statement flows well and covers sufficient facets of the student's activities and interests to explain why they want to study law and why they would be successful in doing so. The only real improvement to be made would be to add discussion of a time the student engaged in academic reading or research into a legal topic beyond what is required of them in their studies.

Personal Statement 5

The way in which the British legal system both reflects and sculpts our constantly changing society fascinates me. Most recently, Tony Nicklinson's fight for the right to die, the pivotal precedent his case set and the legal challenge presented to ethical views exemplified why I want to read and, ultimately, practise law.

The role of the media in extradition cases such as Julian Assange and Abu Qatada, and Helena Kennedy's 'Just Law', made me aware of how extradition can infringe people's rights. The European Arrest Warrant has the ability seriously to undermine the right to freedom, allowing extradition without evidence previously examined in court, as in the case of retired judge Colin Dines, who was extradited to Italy and spent 18 months in jail before coming to trial.

Work placements have widened my interest; a case of suspected fraud at Dickins Hopgood Chidley LLP Solicitors (in which the law was used legitimately) demonstrated the law's ability to restrict a morally correct outcome. This prompted my exploration of jurisprudence, the philosophy of law and varying theories on the link between law and morality. Dworkin's 'Law's Empire' offered particular insight; moral values already exist within the law as unwritten 'principles' and 'policies', but it is judges who ultimately reveal the values to which our legal system is committed. In a recent critical essay discussing the extent to which British moral values are included in our laws, I combined research - such as Finnis' distinctive theory derived from the question of what constitutes a worthwhile, desirable life - with my own evaluations on how morality enters legal decisions, one possibility being the jury.

Observing court procedures and the complexities of different cases (for example, cases of appeal at the Royal Courts of Justice) offered me a first-hand understanding of Dworkin's theory of law as integrity. The intricacies peculiar to each case (such as a case of Count 2 rape re-classified by the Judge as Count 1) the tiers of argument and the clarity of reasoning behind each judgment re-ignited my enthusiasm to pursue a legal career. A Bristol Crown Court trial proved similarly interesting when one defendant changed his plea to guilty, radically affecting the other defendant (pleading not guilty)and requiring one barrister significantly to change his argument. Watching techniques in practice I had learnt during a mock trial at a 'Debate Chamber' master class confirmed how challenging, unpredictable and immediate law can be. It also motivated me to improve vital skills in creating a spontaneous argument without losing the importance of precision and research.

My love for the French language has grown immensely over the past year whilst reading both classical and more modern French novels, particularly enjoying Sagan's 'Bonjour Tristesse' and Claudel's 'La Petite Fille de Monsier Linh'. Work experience at Hill Hofstetter Ltd (with European business links) illustrated how valuable a second language and international awareness is to a law firm; this prompted my search for the opportunity to spend a year in France as part of my degree.

Cross-disciplinary A levels and various co-curricular interests have helped me hone transferable skills well-suited to a law degree. Maths has developed problem-solving and logical aptitudes; analysis of historical sources has advanced my ability to formulate a structured argument, and my knowledge of the genesis of English law. Cicero's 'In Verrem' has heightened my appreciation of the origins of our current legal system, and was made more exciting by comparing ancient techniques to those I witnessed in court, with many (such as speaking directly to the jury) still relevant.

My motivation has always been to maintain top grades alongside involvement in a wide range of activities: I now want to push this academic focus to a higher level and merge all areas of interest into one solid field of specialism and expertise.

Universities applied to:
➤ Oxford: Offer
➤ Durham: Offer
➤ Warwick: Offer
➤ Bristol: Offer
➤ Exeter: Offer

Good Points:

The personal statement opens with a topical example, giving the impression that the student takes interest in legal issues from the outset. Importantly, the introduction is conscious to mention the student's desire to read and practice law – setting up an academic interest from the beginning. The student continues to mention specific legal examples throughout, emphasising this genuine interest. When talking about their legal work experience, the student shows how this progressed back into fostering a specific academic interest in jurisprudence, before then giving what they learned from this study practical application. Such interplay between work experience and academics is highly impressive. The student's current subjects of study are given clear links to law and the punchy ending is effective both stylistically and in emphasising the student's strong personal attributes.

Bad Points:

The only area in which slight improvement could be made is the discussion of the student's French interests. The application is being made to study Law and French Law, and so adding a legal discussion in the paragraph concerning their French interests would have been beneficial.

Overall:

This personal statement is highly impressive. The student capably links everything back to the study or application of law, and this is precisely what will impress academic institutions. The student includes aspects of current legal affairs, specific topics of legal interest, and examples of engaging with law at every available opportunity. It is unsurprising that this personal statement was well-received.

For 95 more example statements and more advice, check the *Ultimate UCAS Personal Statements Guide* – flick to the back to get a free copy.

THE LNAT

THE BASICS

What is the LNAT?

The Law National Admissions Test (LNAT) is a 2 hour and 15-minute written exam for law students who are applying to certain UK universities. It is a computer-based exam that can be sat at different times with unique questions at each sitting. You register to take the test online and book a time slot at a test centre near you.

Test Structure

Section A:

There are 12 passages and 42 questions in the whole of Section A and you have 95 minutes to complete this section. It is a test of your critical thinking and comprehension skills, your ability to identify specific details in large passages and also understand the gist of the passages. It also tests your ability to understand arguments.

Section B:

One essay must be answered from a choice of 3, for which there are 40 minutes to complete. In particular, this tests your ability to construct coherent arguments and to argue persuasively.

Who has to sit the LNAT?

You have to sit the LNAT if you are applying for any of the following universities that ask for it in the current application cycle. You should check this list in May to see if the universities you are considering require it. The following is a list of the universities and courses requiring the LNAT for 2017 entry. As it is subject to change, it is included for guidance only.

University Name	Courses requiring LNAT
University of Birmingham	M100, MR11, MR12, M1N!, M2L6, M240
University of Bristol	M100, MR11, MR12
Durham University	M101, M102
University of Glasgow	M114, M1R7, M1R1, M121, M1R2, M122, M1R3, M1M9, 1RR, M1R4, M123, MN11, MN12, MV13, ML11, MQ13, MQ15, ML17, MV11, MV15, ML12, MR17
Kings College London	LM21, M100, M121, M122, M190
University of Nottingham	M100, M101, M1R1, M1R2
University of Oxford	M100, M190, M191, M192, M193, M194
SOAS, University of London	M100. *M102 (LLB Senior Status) does not require LNAT
University College London	M100, M101, M102, M141, M142, M144, M145, M146

Why is the LNAT used?

The LNAT was established in 2004 and is currently used by a consortium of nine UK universities. Law schools receive highly competitive applications with straight A grades at AS level and strong personal statements. They need to select the best from a pool of the very good applicants they already have and the LNAT fulfils this role.

The LNAT mark and essay are additional pieces of information that are used by admissions tutors when deciding between applicants. They are not used instead of A Levels and GCSEs but merely considered with them.

The multiple choice section examines your critical thinking and verbal reasoning skills, which are very important to do well at the law degree. The LNAT is an aptitude test and while it cannot be studied for, you can very usefully prepare for it. In our experience, it is possible to improve your LNAT score with only a small amount of work and with organised preparation, the results can be fantastic.

Different universities give different weightings to the LNAT. For example, the University of Bristol tends to give a candidate's LNAT a 25% weighting in the admissions decision (with the A Level at 40%, GCSEs at 20% and personal statement at 15%).

When do I sit the LNAT?

Registration for the LNAT normally opens from 1st August online.

You can decide when to sit the LNAT at the time you register for it online. You can choose your date and time slot. While there are available sittings throughout the year, you must sit the LNAT between 1st September through to 20th January for LNAT Universities. You can take the LNAT either before or after you send your UCAS application.

Given the early UCAS application deadline for Oxford University, you must sit the LNAT on or before 20th October in the admissions cycle.

No matter when you take the test, you will not be able to see your result before you send off your UCAS application. Results are issued to candidates in mid-February.

For Oxford:

Registration opens 1 Aug 2016 → Testing begins 1 Sept 2016 → Registration closes 5 Oct 2016 → Testing finishes 20 Oct 2016

For all other universities:

Registration opens 1 Aug 2016 → Testing begins 1 Sept 2016 → Registration closes 15 Jan 2017 → Testing finishes 20 Jan 2017

NB: Please check the dates as they are subject to change every year

How much does it cost?

In 2017, the cost for candidates was £50 at UK or EU test centres. If you are sitting the LNAT at a test centre outside the EU, the cost is £70.

Those candidates who struggle to fund the LNAT may be able to seek an LNAT bursary. This is done via the LNAT consortium's website and you are required to complete an application form online and attach one piece of documentary evidence. This must be done <u>before</u> paying for the test.

If you're a UK applicant, you will be able to claim an LNAT bursary in any of the following circumstances:

➤ Applicants who receive the 16-19 bursary in England, the top rate of EMA (Educational Maintenance Allowance) in Scotland, Wales or Northern Ireland or the Adult Learning Grant
➤ Where you reside with a family member who currently receives either:
   ○ Income support
   ○ Income-based Jobseekers' Allowance
   ○ Employment and Support Allowance
➤ Where you reside with a family member receiving child tax credits + you're named on the award + the household income as stated on the award is less than £30k.
➤ If you receive Pupil Premium payments or free school meals

If you're an EU applicant, you can claim for an LNAT bursary if you receive an equivalent state benefit in your country of residence.

If you're outside the EU, you are not eligible for an LNAT bursary.

Can I re-sit the LNAT?

You cannot resit the LNAT in the same application cycle. Whatever score you get is with you for the year. That's why it's so important to make sure you're well prepared and ready to perform at your very best on the test day.

If I reapply, do I have to resit the LNAT?

Yes. If you apply in a different admissions cycle then you need to retake the LNAT and the score from your new test will be sent to universities.

When do I get my results?

If you sit the LNAT by the 20th January deadline, you will receive your results by email in early February 2017. You will just receive your score of Section A and the average score for the cohort in the admissions cycle.

Section B is not marked by Pearson but is in fact marked by the universities' admissions tutors themselves. Accordingly, you will not get a mark back on Section B (but it is still taken into account in the admissions process)

Where do I sit the LNAT?

You can sit the LNAT at any Pearson test centre – these are the computer test centres where the driving theory test is taken. Once you book the test, you can choose the most convenient test centre to sit it at.

How is the LNAT scored?

Once you finish the test, your score is calculated by the computer. For all tests taken before 20th October, the universities that require the LNAT will receive the result directly from the test provider on the 21st October. On any day after 20th October, your test result will be sent directly to the LNAT universities within 24 hours of you taking the test.

Section A: Is scored out of 42 and the average score tends to vary from year to year, depending on the difficulty of the test. There are no mark deductions for incomplete or incorrect answers, so it's a good idea to answer every question even if it's a guess.

Section B: Your essay is sent directly to the universities and they will mark it themselves. They are testing your ability to construct a reasoned, persuasive and balanced argument, and to write in cogent English. There is a lot of essay writing at degree level, so Section B is a vital part of the LNAT.

How is the LNAT used?

The weighting which the universities place on the LNAT varies. The University of Bristol, for example, place a 25% weighting on it. The universities use the LNAT for a reason and place a lot of importance on both Section A and B. Therefore, the better you do at the LNAT, the better your chances of securing an offer. Given how competitive the law admissions process is, it is vital to produce a solid score on the LNAT. Each university will offer its own guidance on the LNAT on their admissions website.

How does my score compare?

This completely depends on how tough the test is and thus, the average scores. The average tends to vary each year but in the 2015-16 admissions cycle, the average mark for Section A was 23.3 out of 42.

Access Arrangements

If you need extra time, medication in the exam or any other special arrangement for the exam, you must apply with the Examination Access Requirements form, which is available from the LNAT website. It is important to apply before you book the test and it is necessary to attach evidence demonstrating your eligibility.

If you ordinarily receive extra time in public examinations, you would likely be granted it for the LNAT.

General Advice

Practice

Preparing for the LNAT will certainly improve your LNAT score. You won't be familiar with the type of questions in the LNAT and answering such questions in timed conditions. With practice, you'll become significantly quicker in reading the passages in Section A and your speed will increase greatly. Practice will also help you learn and hone techniques to improve your accuracy. This will make you calm and composed on test day, allowing you to perform at your best.

Start Early

It is easier to prepare if you practice little and often – this will be much more effective than just looking at practice questions on the night before the test. So start your preparation well in advance, ideally by August. This way, you will have a lot of time to work through practice questions to build up your speed and incorporate time-saving techniques into your approach. How to start? Well, by reading this you're obviously on track!

How to Work

It is necessary to focus on both Section A and Section B in your preparation. Even though you only get a score for Section A, universities place significant weight on Section B.

Section A:

It would be worth reading about the section and then going through a passage in your own time and understand what the questions are asking for. In particular, it would be useful to understand how an argument works by reading about the advice for Section A in this book. This will help you identify arguments in passages.

Even going through one passage and its set of questions per day would be worthwhile preparation whilst going through the worked solutions to any questions you answered incorrectly.

Closer to the test day, you would need to work in timed conditions, which is approximately 8 minutes per passage in order to become comfortable working under pressure. It is particularly important in the LNAT to be able to get the main idea or argument of the passage as a whole but to also focus on the details. Practice on Section A type questions will invariably make you faster.

Section B:

This is a very important part of the LNAT. A complaint of an admissions tutor when the LNAT first came out was that many candidates were unable to write a reasoned argument. So it would be worthwhile reading through the advice for Section B in this book and then to go about writing answers to topics you're unfamiliar with (as well as the examples given in this book). This will help you feel comfortable writing in exam conditions.

Crucially, Section B requires a broad range of knowledge and could involve any area of general knowledge. However, the main skill being assessed is your ability to construct a reasoned and persuasive argument, which is a vital skill for a law degree. Indeed, it would be worth getting a second person to take a look at a sample essay (such as an English/History A Level teacher). Even if you think you are fine writing essays in A Levels, writing an essay on an unfamiliar topic can sometimes unnerve people and the best way to overcome this is practice.

Repeat Tough Questions

When checking through answers, pay particular attention to questions you have got wrong. Look closely through the worked answers in this book until you're confident you understand the reasoning - then repeat the question later without help to check you can now do it. If you use other resources where only the answer is given, have another look at the question and consider showing it to a friend or teacher for their opinion.

Statistics show that without consolidating and reviewing your mistakes, you're likely to make the same mistakes again. Don't be a statistic. Look back over your mistakes and address the cause to make sure you don't make similar mistakes when it comes to the test. You should avoid guessing in early practice. Highlight any questions you struggled with so you can go back and improve.

Positive Marking

There is no negative marking in the LNAT – marking is only positive and you won't lose points for making a wrong answer. Therefore, if you aren't able to answer a question, you should guess.

For each question, there are 5 possible answers, thereby giving you a 20% chance of guessing correctly. If you need to guess, see if you can eliminate some of the options as this will improve your chances of making a successful guess.

Booking your Test

If you're applying to Oxford, it's necessary to take the test before the 20th October. It makes no difference what day you take it on as the results of all test results taken between the 1st September and 20th October are only sent to universities on the 21st October. That said, it would be best not to leave it too late in case of unforeseen circumstances, such as illness.

For all other universities, you just need to take the test before the 20th January. While it would be preferable not to leave it to the last minute, it is not necessary to do it in September or even before the 20th October. It would be much better to ensure that you're comfortable with the LNAT and have completed as much practice as possible. This would stand you in good stead for a solid LNAT result.

Mock Test

There are two full LNAT papers freely available at www.lnat.ac.uk and it would be worth going through them in timed conditions after you have worked through the questions in this book. There are also a further two full mock papers available at **www.uniadmissions.co.uk/lnat-past-papers**

A word on timing...

"If you had all day to do your LNAT, you would get 100%. But you don't."

Whilst this isn't completely true, it illustrates a very important point. Once you've practiced and know how to answer the questions, the clock is your biggest enemy. This seemingly obvious statement has one very important consequence. **The way to improve your LNAT score is to improve your speed.** There is no magic bullet. But there are a great number of techniques that, with practice, will give you significant time gains, allowing you to answer more questions and score more marks.

Timing is tight throughout the LNAT – **mastering timing is the first key to success**. Some candidates choose to work as quickly as possible to save up time at the end to check back, but this is generally not the best way to do it. LNAT questions can have a lot of information in them – each time you start answering a question it takes time to get familiar with the instructions and information. By splitting the question into two sessions (the first run-through and the return-to-check) you double the amount of time you spend on familiarising yourself with the data, as you have to do it twice instead of only once. This costs valuable time. In addition, candidates who do check back may spend 2–3 minutes doing so and yet not make any actual changes. Whilst this can be reassuring, it is a false reassurance as it is unlikely to have a significant effect on your actual score. Therefore, it is usually best to pace yourself very steadily, aiming to spend the same amount of time on each question and finish the final question in a section just as time runs out. This reduces the time spent on re-familiarising with questions and maximises the time spent on the first attempt, gaining more marks.

It is essential that you don't get stuck with the hardest questions – no doubt there will be some. In the time spent answering only one of these, you may miss out on answering three easier questions. If a question is taking too long, choose a sensible answer and move on. Never see this as giving up or in any way failing, rather it is the smart way to approach a test with a tight time limit. With practice and discipline, you can get very good at this and learn to maximise your efficiency. It is not about being a hero and aiming for full marks – this is almost impossible and very much unnecessary. It is about maximising your efficiency and gaining the maximum possible number of marks within the time you have.

Top tip! Ensure that you take a watch that can show you the time in seconds into the exam. This will allow you have a much more accurate idea of the time you're spending on a question. In general, if you've spent more than 9 minutes on a section A passage – move on regardless of how close you think you are to finishing it.

SECTION A

Section A is the multiple choice section. In the exam, you will be presented with 12 passages and 42 questions, with approximately 3-4 questions per passage. There is a total of 95 minutes for this section and you cannot use any of the time for Section B in Section A – you only have a maximum of 95 minutes.

The aim of this section is to test the following skills:

➢ Comprehension
➢ Interpretation
➢ Deduction

This tests your ability to understand the different parts of a passage. It is important to understand what constitutes a good argument:

1. **Evidence:** Arguments which are heavily based on value judgements and subjective statements tend to be weaker than those based on facts, statistics and the available evidence.
2. **Logic**: A good argument should flow and the constituent parts should fit well into an overriding view or belief.
3. **Balance:** A good argument must concede that there are other views or beliefs (counter-argument). The key is to carefully dismantle these ideas and explain why they are wrong.

Sometimes, the question requires you to consider whether an argument is 'strong' or 'weak'. All arguments include reasons (premises) which aim to support a conclusion. Here, we are considering whether the reasons provide weak or strong support.

The parts of an argument:

An argument is an untimely attempt to persuade with the use of reasons. This can be distinguished from an assertion, which is simply a statement of fact or belief.

Assertion: It is raining outside.

Argument: I can hear the continuous sound of water splashing on the roof. Therefore, it must be raining outside.

The argument involves an attempt to persuade another that it is raining and it includes a reason as to why the speaker thinks it is raining, which is the splashing on the roof. The assertion, on the other hand, is not backed up with a reason – it is simply a statement.

An argument involves a premise and a conclusion.

A premise is simply a statement from which another can be inferred or follows as a conclusion.

A conclusion though is a summary of the arguments made.

For example:

Premise 1: All dogs bark.

Premise 2: My pet is a dog.

Conclusion: My pet barks.

The conclusion here follows from both of the premises.

Explanation

Sometimes, it will be necessary to distinguish an argument from an explanation and you will need to be careful here as it can be difficult to distinguish sometimes. In essence, an argument will always involve an attempt to persuade the reader as to a point of view. Explanations, on the other hand, do not. Explanations may describe why something is the way it is or account for how something has occurred.

For example:

1. **Explanation:** We can hear the sound of water drops because the tap is leaking.
2. **Argument:** We can hear the sound of water drops. Therefore, we need to call the plumber.

Example 1 just accounts for *why* water drops can be heard – there is no attempt to persuade the reader that there are either water drops or that the tap is leaking. The tap leaking is just asserted as an explanation for the sound of the water drops.

In example 2, the author is advancing an argument as the author is making the case to call the plumber. The premise being the sound of water drops.

Premise vs. Conclusion

- A **Conclusion** is a summary of the arguments being made and is usually explicitly stated or heavily implied.
- A **Premise** is a statement from which another statement can be inferred or follows as a conclusion.

Hence, a conclusion is shown/implied/proven by a premise. Similarly, a premise shows/indicates/establishes a conclusion. Consider for example: *My mom, being a woman, is clever as all women are clever.*

Premise 1: My mom is a woman + **Premise 2:** Women are clever = **Conclusion:** My mom is clever.

This is fairly straightforward as it's a very short passage and the conclusion is explicitly stated. Sometimes the latter may not happen. Consider: *My mom is a woman and all women are clever.*

Here, whilst the conclusion is not explicitly being stated, both premises still stand and can be used to reach the same conclusion.

You may sometimes be asked to identify if any of the options cannot be "reliably concluded". This is effectively asking you to identify why an option **cannot** be the conclusion. There are many reasons why but the most common ones are:

1. Over-generalising: *My mom is clever therefore all women are clever.*
2. Being too specific: *All kids like candy thus my son also likes candy.*
3. Confusing Correlation vs. Causation: *Lung cancer is much more likely in patients who drink water. Hence, water causes lung cancer.*
4. Confusing Cause and Effect: *Lung cancer patients tend to smoke so it follows that having lung cancer must make people want to smoke.*

Note how conjunctives like hence, thus, therefore, and it follows, give you a clue as to when a conclusion is being stated. More examples of these include: "it follows that, implies that, whence, entails that".

Similarly, words like "because, as indicated by, in that, given that, due to the fact that" usually identify premises.

Assumptions

It is important to be able to identify assumptions in a passage as questions frequently ask to identify these.

An assumption is a reasonable assertion that can be made based on the available evidence.

A crucial difference between an assumption and a premise is that a premise is normally mentioned in the passage, whereas an assumption is not. A useful way to consider whether there is a particular assumption in the passage is to consider whether the conclusion relies on it to work – i.e. if the assumption is taken away, does that affect the conclusion? If it does, then it's an assumption.

> *Top tip!* Don't get confused between premises and assumptions. A **premise** is a statement that is explicitly stated in the passage. An **assumption** is an inference that is made from the passage.

Fact vs. Opinion

Sometimes you will be required to distinguish between a fact and an opinion. A fact is something that can be tested to be true or false. An opinion, on the other hand, cannot be tested to be true or false – it is someone's view on something and is a value judgement.

For example: "Tuition fees were reduced by the Welsh government in 2012. Many viewed this as a fair outcome."

Fact: Tuition fees were reduced by the Welsh government.

Opinion: It is a fair outcome.

What one person sees as being 'fair' may not be 'fair' to another person – even if many people see a particular policy as fair. It is a normative statement that cannot be tested as true or false.

> *Top tip!* Though it might initially sound counter-intuitive, it is often best to read the question *before* reading the passage. Then you'll have a much better idea of what you're looking for and are therefore more likely to find it quicker.

Correlation vs. Causation

Just because two incidents or events have occurred does not mean that one has caused the other. For example: "French people are known for having a glass of wine with dinner and they have a larger life expectancy than we do. Therefore, we should consume wine to be healthier."

This argument is flawed. There are 2 events: (i) French people known for having wine and (ii) French people having a larger life expectancy. There is no suggestion in the extract that (i) wine is causally related to (ii) or that having wine actually leads to a longer life. Accordingly, in itself, the premises do not adequately support the conclusion – there could be other reasons such as diet or exercise.

Approaching Section A

Responses

For each question, there are 5 options to choose from. Only one can be correct. Therefore, if you cannot find the correct one initially, you can use the process of elimination to find the correct one.

If you are stuck on a particular passage or question, do not spend too long on it as this can take time away from your other questions. It would be best to leave it until the end if you have time left.

The Passage

Take every fact in the passage as true and your answer must be based on the information in the passage only – so do not use your own knowledge, even if you feel that you personally know the topic. For example, if the question asks who the first person was to walk on the moon, then states "the three crew members of the first lunar mission were Edwin Aldrin, Neil Armstrong, and Michael Collins". The correct answer is "cannot tell" – even though you know it was Neil Armstrong and see his name, the passage itself does not tell you who left the landing craft first. Likewise, if there is a quotation or an extract from a book which is factually inaccurate, you should answer based on the information available to you rather than what you know to be true.

Read the Questions First

Different strategies work well for different people but indeed, having a look at the questions before going through the passage can help you focus on the important details in the passage in the first reading of it, thereby saving you time.

It would be best to try this strategy with some of the passages in this book to see if it works for you.

Timing

Even if you finish the questions before the 95 minutes runs out, you **cannot** use any of this extra time on Section B – you can only use this 95 minutes on Section A so you might as well go back through any questions that you found difficult or whether you were uncertain in any areas.

Knowledge

No knowledge is required for Section A and no knowledge of the law or current affairs is required.

Reading Non-Fiction

As well as critically analysing the passages in the book, a brilliant preparation for the LNAT is to engage in further non-fiction reading and to consider some of the following questions:

➢ What issues are being raised?
➢ What assumptions are made?
➢ What is the conclusion?
➢ Is there adequate support for the conclusion?
➢ Whose perspective is it coming from?
➢ How would you create a counter-argument?

Critically reading non-fiction, such as in a quality newspaper, will not only help improve your Section A performance but would also improve your knowledge bank for the Section B essay.

SECTION A QUESTIONS

Passage 1 – Controlled Drugs

There is a consensus among Parliamentarians that the current drug policy is simply not working. Approximately 1 in 12 adults in the UK have taken an illicit drug in the last year (amounting to 2.8 million people) and 1 in 5 young adults have taken an illicit drug. It is thus clear that the Government needs to do more. However, while it is clear that there needs to be a shift in policy, politicians cannot agree on what changes are needed.

Possessing a banned drug is a criminal offence but how can it be that all these individuals are potentially criminals? Is it moral to label these individuals as criminals? Around the world, there have been growing calls for the legalisation of drugs. In 2001, Portugal legislated to decriminalise the use of small amounts of drugs. Since then, drug consumption in Portugal has been below the European average and the percentage of young people aged 15-24 consuming drugs in Portugal has decreased. It is clear that the legalisation of drugs has not had the effect that opponents of the policy claimed it would have. Accordingly, decriminalising drugs may be a pointer in the right direction for the UK.

A key justification for criminalising the possession of drugs is that it would reduce the propensity of drug consumption (or deter people from consuming drugs). However, there is no strong evidence to support this notion. Once a person is in possession of a controlled drug, they have committed a criminal offence, yet this has not deterred the 2.8 million users. Further, a study by the European Union's Drugs Monitoring Agency found no correlation between harsher punishments for drug offences and lower drug consumption. This makes the argument for legalisation much more compelling.

Moreover, drug consumption in itself is a victimless crime in that it doesn't harm anyone apart from the drug user. Furthermore, the majority of users only consume drugs in small amounts which are unlikely to harm themselves. Any negative health effects that can be incurred are limited to the individual. This is in contrast to smoking, where 'passive smoking' can have a serious impact on others.

Opponents of legalisation have suggested that a drug addiction can lead to other crimes, such as theft and robbery, as the individual resorts to secondary crimes to fund their expensive addiction. Accordingly, they argue that taking controlled drugs can be criminogenic. However, this misses the point. The underlying reason for which individuals participate in such secondary crimes (e.g. robbery or theft) is the very high prices of controlled drugs, which are, in turn, a consequence of their prohibition. The very fact that they are illegal means that only criminal gangs end up supplying the controlled drugs, leading to the high prices. If the prohibition is removed, the increase in supply would reduce the price of the drugs and thus, reduce the 'need' to resort to crimes such as theft or robbery.

Legalisation is preferable to criminalisation but that is not to say that legalisation alone would suffice. Excess drug use should be seen as a public health issue, rather than a problem for the criminal law. While a drug addiction can lead to medical issues, so too can excess alcohol. Is it not incoherent for a society to allow any amount of alcohol consumption and yet totally prohibit the smallest consumption of controlled drugs? Accordingly, the freedom that individuals have to choose whether to consume alcohol should be accorded to them in regard to drugs.

1. What is the meaning of **criminogenic** in its context in this passage?
   A. That consuming a controlled drug is a crime
   B. That taking controlled drugs can lead to other crimes being committed
   C. That taking controlled drugs is a victimless crime
   D. That criminalisation is not the best response to reduce the consumption of drugs
   E. Crimes such as theft or robbery

2. Which of the following is presented as being *paradoxical* by the author?
   A. That smoking is not prohibited and yet drugs are prohibited
   B. That alcohol is not prohibited and yet drugs are prohibited
   C. That drug consumption is a victimless crime
   D. That it is not drugs per se that lead to robbery or theft but the high prices of the drugs
   E. That a justification for criminalising drugs is to reduce the consumption of drugs but there is no strong evidence to support that point

3. What is the main argument in the passage?
   A. Drug use is a public health issue, rather than a problem for the criminal law
   B. Drug consumption is victimless
   C. Drug consumption is not criminogenic
   D. That controlled drugs should be regulated
   E. That controlled drugs should be legalised

4. What practical effect does the author believe would come about if the consumption of drugs were legalised?
   A. Drug consumption would fall
   B. Drug consumption would increase
   C. Drug users would take part in fewer secondary crimes (such as robbery and theft)
   D. It makes society fairer
   E. Drug use would be seen as a public health issue

5. Which of the following would most weaken the author's main argument?
   A. Drug consumption has a tendency to increase one's propensity for violence
   B. Criminalisation is moral
   C. Drugs have more negative health effects than alcohol
   D. Drug dealers could turn to other crimes – such as people trafficking
   E. It is not clear that there isn't a deterrent effect of criminalisation

Passage 2 – Sweeney Todd

Despite the fact that some associate musicals with cheesy joy, the genre is not limited to gleeful stories, as can be demonstrated by the macabre musical, 'Sweeney Todd'. The original story of the murderous barber appears in a Victorian penny dreadful, 'The String of Pearls: A Romance'. The penny dreadful material was adapted for the 19th century stage, and in the 20th century was adapted into two separate melodramas, before the story was taken up by Stephen Sondheim and Hugh Wheeler. The pair turned it into a new musical, which has since been performed across the globe and been adapted into a film starring Johnny Depp.

Sondheim and Wheeler's drama tells a disturbing narrative: the protagonist, falsely accused of a crime by a crooked judge, escapes from Australia to be told that his wife was raped by that same man of the court. In response, she has committed suicide, and her daughter - Todd's daughter - has been made the ward of the judge. The eponymous figure ultimately goes on a killing spree, vowing vengeance against the people who have wronged him but also declaring 'we all deserve to die', and acting on this belief by killing many of his clients; men who come to his barbershop. His new partner in crime, Mrs Lovett, comes up with the idea of turning the bodies of his victims into the filling of pies, as a way of sourcing affordable meat - after all, she claims, 'times is hard'.

Cannibalism, vengeance, murder, and corruption - these are all themes that demonstrate that this show does not conform to a happy-clappy preconception of its genre.

Sondheim and Wheeler's musical has been adapted into a number of formats over the years, including the film 'Sweeney Todd: The Demon Barber of Fleet Street' directed by Tim Burton. The nature of a film production necessitated a number of changes to the musical. Burton even acknowledged that while it was based on the musical, they were out to make a film and not a Broadway show. Accordingly, a three-hour musical was cut into a two-hour film, which brought a number of challenges: some of the songs and the romance between Todd's daughter and Anthony (a sailor) had to be removed.

There was initially concern though as the film actors, while critically acclaimed in their profession, were not professional singers. However, that turned out to be a non-issue as the film's soundtrack received glowing reviews, in particular, Depp's voice which received positive critical appraisals.

6. Which of the following statements are best supported by the above passage?
   A. Sondheim is a brilliant musician and lyricist
   B. Most musicals deal with morbid themes
   C. Wheeler is an avid penny dreadful fan
   D. Generalisations can be misleading
   E. Film adaptations lead to fundamental changes in the storyline

7. All the adjectives below are explicitly supported by the passage as ways of describing the crimes described within it, except:
   A. Comic
   B. Culinary
   C. Vengeful
   D. Sexual
   E. Disturbing

8. Which of the following statements best sums up Todd's belief?
   A. Bad people should die so good can live and prosper
   B. Good people should die because the bad have basically taken over
   C. All men should die
   D. All humans merit death
   E. Death is unavoidable

9. Which of the following statements is best supported in the above passage?
   A. There are four themes in 'Sweeney Todd'
   B. Legal corruption is the predominate theme of 'Sweeney Todd'
   C. Several 'Sweeney Todd' themes are morbid
   D. There is nothing positive in 'Sweeney Todd'
   E. Sadness is the focus of Sweeny Todd

10. Which of the following is true?
    A. Mrs Lovett and Sweeney Todd are in a romantic relationship
    B. All of the songs from the musical were removed or adjusted
    C. The storyline of the film adaptation was fundamentally different to the musical
    D. The film did not receive positive critical acclaim
    E. The film actors did not have professional musical experience

Passage 3 – Youth Unemployment

Youth Unemployment -that is: those young people who are in search of work but are unable to get into work -is disturbingly high. The current youth unemployment figure for the UK is at an unsettling 12%. This is much higher than that of other developed countries such as Germany and Switzerland and the societal implications of this are greater than what the politicians acknowledge. The longer a young person is unemployed, the less likely they are to find a job at all. This has destructive effects on the country: it increases the government's spending on welfare pay-outs, reduces the economy's capacity and increases the likelihood of crime. The personal impact of youth unemployment is equally devastating; lower quality of life, low self-esteem, and lack of confidence and even depression, which can lead to a never-ending cycle of unemployment. It is, thus, clear that youth unemployment is a dangerous virus that demands immediate government attention.

There are a number of reasons for the high youth unemployment rate, such as the sluggish state of the economy and the global financial crash in 2007/08. When the economy is not doing well, businesses tend to lay off workers in response to a lack of sales. This happened in 2008 when the economy slumped and unemployment drastically increased. Since then, the economy has only recovered lethargically.

However, this alone does not account for the entirety of the youth unemployment rate. Since the economic slump of 2008, total unemployment has reduced to 5.4%, while youth unemployment is at a much higher 12%. Why is there such a big difference? Is it just an inherent feature of society? Do businesses not want young people? A number of young people report that there aren't enough jobs for them. Yet at the same time, businesses say they are desperate to find skilled young people. They just can't find young people with the right skills to suit their needs. For example, Dulux, the paint manufacturer, has pointed out that there simply aren't enough skilled painters and decorators. In London, two-thirds of construction firms have had to turn down work as they don't have enough practical and skilled workers. And herein lies the problem – many young people do not have the skills that businesses are looking for.

That is not to say that it is the fault of those who are unemployed. The root of the problem is the lack of courses that are geared to the kind of skills that businesses want and the existing structural inadequacies within our education system. The head of Ofsted recently pointed out that the lack of high-quality vocational courses in England is a concern. Vocational courses have traditionally been seen as a 'second-rate' option in the country, with the academic A Levels being the 'gold' standard. This view must change – not everyone is destined for academia and vocationally trained individuals have an important role in our society. Would you rather have a well-read English graduate or a vocationally trained engineer fix your central heating? Thus, the government must make high-quality vocational provision a priority. Vocational education tends to be incorrectly seen as second-rate by students and this must change. Putting an emphasis on vocational courses will address the skills shortage in the UK, make the UK more productive, and crucially improve the prospects of our young generation. In addition, the education sector and businesses should engage with each other more closely to ensure that skill deficits are addressed in the national curriculum.

A report from the Institute for Public Policy Research (IPPR) suggests that youth unemployment tends to be lower in countries where there is a vocational route into employment and not just an academic one. This shines a lot of light on the situation in the UK.

11. Which of the following is **not** a potential personal impact of youth unemployment?
    A. Lower quality of life
    B. Increases the government's spending on welfare pay-outs
    C. Lack of confidence
    D. Low self-esteem
    E. Depression

12. Which of the following is the underlying reason for the high youth unemployment rate?
    A. The global financial crash of 2007/08
    B. Not enough jobs for young people
    C. Lack of skills
    D. The head of Ofsted
    E. The lack of high-quality vocational courses

13. Which of the following is implied but **not** stated in the passage?
    A. There is a mismatch between the skills that young people have and the skills that employers are looking for
    B. Young people don't have the skills that businesses are looking for
    C. Teachers should encourage young people to undertake vocational courses
    D. Businesses should provide training to improve the skills of young people
    E. Unemployment is bad

14. Which of the following is the author's main argument in the passage?
    A. An increased emphasis should be placed on vocational courses
    B. An increase in the skills of young people needs to be brought about
    C. Better jobs for young people are needed
    D. That unemployment has caused a lack of skills
    E. That there aren't enough skilled young people

15. According to the author, what can businesses do to reduce youth unemployment?
    A. Create more jobs
    B. Increase young people's skills
    C. Engage with the education sector
    D. Train more young people
    E. Create vocational courses

Passage 4 – The English Reformation

In the early 1500s, King Henry VIII set the English Church on a different course forever. Henry was undoubtedly a devout catholic when he took the throne. Indeed, he was a staunch defender of Catholicism in the face of threats from religious reformers, such as Luther. Impressed by Henry VIII's defence, the Pope gave him the title 'Defender of the Faith'. So how did Henry come to separate from the Roman Church?

Although historians are not universally in agreement, many put Henry VIII as the key driver behind separating the Church of England from Rome. Henry was disappointed in his marriage with Catherine of Aragon as, in spite of multiple pregnancies, they only had one daughter together. Henry though was desperate to conceive a son. He had a monumental ego and was, thus, concerned about his legacy. In order to secure his dynasty and ensure that the Tudor reign remained strong, he needed a legitimate son. Accordingly, he was eager to secure a divorce with his current wife and marry Anne Boleyn with the aim of having a legitimate son with her. The English church was under the authority of the Roman Catholic Church (of whom the Pope was the leader) and in order to separate from Catherine, Henry needed to obtain an annulment from the Pope. Despite the mammoth efforts of Henry's right-hand man, he was unable to secure an annulment of the marriage from Rome, which would have been the straightforward option. It became clear that Rome was not going to budge on this and from then, Henry began to pursue a separation from the Roman Church.

Historians also point to another reason for Henry's desire to break away from Rome. He liked the idea of being the only head of the church and the supreme leader. His ego influenced many of his key decisions, such as engaging in wars abroad, and this decision was no different.

A number of historians suggest that Thomas Cromwell was the man behind the separation. Indeed, Cromwell played a significant role in engineering it. With control of the King's parliamentary affairs, he persuaded Parliament to enact a supplication pronouncing Henry as 'the only head' of the church, establishing the doctrine of royal supremacy. This was in clear conflict with Papal authority and began the process of breaking away from the Roman Church. But while it is clear that Cromwell had a vital role in the break from Rome, the obvious must still be repeated – were it not for Henry's desire of a break, there would not have been such a break.

Through a series of Acts of Parliament over two years, the break from Rome was secured and ties between the English church and Rome were severed. One such Act of Parliament in 1934, the Act of Supremacy, declared the King as 'the only Supreme head in earth of the Church of England.' This drastic change put the English church on a new course and while there were no major day-to-day changes initially, it planted the seed for the differences we see today between the Roman Catholic Church and the Church of England.

16. What was the ultimate cause of the Church of England's breakaway from Rome?
    A. Henry VIII's ego
    B. Rome wouldn't grant him a divorce
    C. Henry wanted a son
    D. Royal Supremacy
    E. Religious reasons

17. What does 'dynasty' mean in the Passage?
    A. Family
    B. Henry's control of the Kingdom
    C. Succession of people from Henry's family to the throne
    D. Exertion of dominion by the Tudors
    E. The power of Henry VIII

18. Why did Henry want a son?
    A. To secure Royal Supremacy
    B. He wanted to divorce Catherine
    C. To secure the Tudor reign
    D. Males were preferred in the 16th Century
    E. None of the above

19. Which of the following is an unstated assumption?
    A. Henry had an ego
    B. There was no opposition to the reformation
    C. The public was supportive of the break from Rome
    D. Henry needed Cromwell to make the break from Rome
    E. Henry believed that he couldn't get a divorce through Rome

20 What is the Royal Supremacy?
    A. The breaking away from Rome
    B. The idea of the King being the supreme authority
    C. The King becoming the leader of the church
    D. The authority of the Pope over the Church
    E. The Act of Supremacy 1934

Passage 5 – Charities and Public Schools

What constitutes a charity is a matter of public significance, but also an important issue in determining the taxable income a charity receives. In the popular sense, charities are seen as institutions which primarily help the poor, however, a question has been raised as to why public schools should be considered as charities considering the fees required to attend them.

In order to be classified and registered as a charity, it is necessary for an institution to demonstrate that its purposes are for the public benefit. Once accorded charity status, the institution gains a number of fiscal benefits from the government. For example, no corporation tax is paid on most types of income. In contrast, corporation tax, which currently stands at 20% of all profits, is paid by all other private businesses. The law should not allow a 'free-for-all' where any profit-making company can be a charity by just doing a minuscule charitable act, as this would have a negative impact on the public purse. Nonetheless, charitable status is highly sought out by many organisations for these reasons and has become highly controversial in the case of public schools.

Public schools charge a fee for admission, in contrast with state schools, which are funded by the Government. Accordingly, as public schools are private institutions, becoming charitable will help their finances. Whether this should be possible hinges on what acting for the public benefit means and requires in the context of education.

In 2011, the Independent Schools Council (ISC), representing public schools, sought a judicial review of the Charity Commission's guidance on what is required for a public school to demonstrate a 'public benefit'. The ISC argued that they did provide a public benefit, but they did face opposition. The Education Review Group, who helped draft the Commission's disputed guidance, also intervened in the case, advancing arguments in the trial. Ultimately, the tribunal held that the Commission's guidance was wrong as a matter of law and required them to change it. The trial judge decided that in order to operate for the public benefit, a sufficient section of society must directly benefit from the education provided, which he said must include children whose parents would be unable to afford the fees without assistance.

In the trial, a number of arguments were advanced on either side of the issue. One such argument was that independent schools are a net cost to society as they remove able pupils from state schools and present barriers to social mobility. However, the tribunal did not consider such an argument as it related to a 'political' issue, rather than a judicial one.

Further, private education provision can provide a multitude of benefits to society. Indeed, it educates the children whose parents pay for the provision. While this may not seem inherently charitable because parents are paying for the education, there are public benefits too. Firstly, the provision of education in itself is a benefit – having an educated population benefits not only the individuals through enabling them to enjoy a higher living standard, but also the general economy. More taxes will be paid and there will be less crime. That is not to say that we should ignore the gap between public schools and state schools. Indeed, state schools that are struggling should be willing to receive help from public schools and public schools should, in accordance with their public duty, offer such help.

21. Which of the following is definitely true based on the passage?
    A. Any institution that provides a public benefit gains fiscal benefits from the government
    B. Every organisation would rather be a charity than a private company
    C. If an organisation is not a charity, it does not provide a public benefit
    D. Charities may not have to pay corporation tax
    E. The law should not allow a free-for-all

22. Which of the following is required if an organisation is to become a charity?
    A. To help the poor
    B. Nothing
    C. To exist for the public good
    D. To demonstrate that the fiscal benefits gained would be for the public benefit
    E. To not make private profits

23. Who is most likely to have advanced the argument that public schools are a net cost to society based on the passage?
    A. The Independent Schools Council
    B. The tribunal judges
    C. State schools
    D. The Education Review Group
    E. The government

24. Which of the following is an opinion as opposed to a fact?
    A. The tribunal did not consider the argument that there was a net cost to society
    B. No corporation tax is paid on most types of income
    C. Public schools charge a fee for admission
    D. The law should not allow a free-for-all
    E. A charity has to demonstrate that it operates for the public benefit

25. Which of the following would have adequately supported the argument that there is a public benefit from public schools before the tribunal?
    A. Public schools educate the children whose parents pay for it
    B. Public schools provide scholarships to others who can't afford the fees
    C. Public schools can make better use of money, as opposed to it being paid through tax
    D. Public schools are better than state schools
    E. State schools can learn from public schools

Passage 6 – Amazon vs. Hachette

The public does not normally witness corporate trade negotiations or disputes. They are generally held behind closed doors and in private for the mutual benefit of the companies in the dispute. However, there was an exception in the dispute between the international publisher, Hachette, and Amazon in 2014. Both of them are powerful organisations with market power, however, this episode has shown that one is more powerful than the other.

It is first necessary to go into the background of this dispute. The sale of a book involves three main protagonists. Arguably the most important, the author writes the book. The publisher prints and distributes the book. The retailers then act as the point of sale to consumers. In the US, there are five very large publishers who have enjoyed significant market dominance. When distributing their books, publishers want them in the biggest retailers and crucially, the biggest of them all by far is Amazon. It is estimated by some that 50% of all book sales (both printed and electronic) across the US go through Amazon. It is the most dominant bookseller and, therefore, it is imperative for publishers to get their books on Amazon. In order to do this though, each publisher needs to enter into a legal contract with Amazon, which is normally a private arrangement.

In 2014, Hachette and Amazon were in negotiations to renew their contract for the pricing and distribution of Hachette's books. While the exact issues in the negotiations remain private, it became clear that the negotiations weren't going well. Amazon stopped selling a number of Hachette's books and delayed deliveries of many by weeks. Famous books such as those by *JK Rowling* were delayed. Was this just business? Or did Amazon go too far? It infuriated both Hachette and the authors of the books that Hachette publish. It showed the length that Amazon would go to in order to get what they want. Hachette's authors, who normally stayed out of publisher-retailer contracts, weighed in and criticised Amazon. Amazon had used their enormous market power to restrict the sales of the books from Hachette to try to get their way and many authors argued that Amazon had abused their market power. However, it was only a minority of authors (and mainly the successful ones) that spoke out.

In reality, Hachette and their authors are not the innocent victims in all of this. Hachette, with their market power in publishing, conspired with the other major US publishers and Apple to fix the prices of eBooks (i.e. to keep them artificially high) in 2012. When the US Department of Justice sued, the publishers (including Hachette) made a settlement for $164m. So it's a bit rich for Hachette to complain about Amazon's aggressive price strategy.

In regard to individual authors, the major publishers haven't always been friendly either. It is a monstrous task for an up and coming author to get even a small book deal with a publisher. Publishers generally have a narrow view as to what a suitable book is and are primarily focused on what they think the monetary returns will be. Amazon, though, has taken a new step. They have introduced a suite of services that allows authors to self-publish their work through Amazon. It allows individuals to publish both an eBook and a print book. Amazon, with their vast resources, are also able to offer a 'print-on-demand' service whereby Amazon prints each book to order. This bypasses the need for traditional publishers or any need for a large pot of cash to fund a print run. Surely, this genius innovation should be applauded. It allows many more small-time authors to self-publish their works and disrupts the unfairness that the big publishers created. Yes, Amazon has excessive market power, but at least they're using it to the benefit of small authors, unlike the traditional publishers. So let them engage in whatever tactics they want to with Hachette.

26. What is the author's view as to the balance of power between Amazon and Hachette?
    A. Hachette is more powerful than Amazon
    B. Amazon is more powerful than Hachette
    C. They are both powerful
    D. The author doesn't have a view as to which
    E. They have both exerted market power

27. The author stated that it is 'a bit rich for Hachette to complain about Amazon's aggressive strategy'. What is he suggesting about Hachette's complaint?
    A. It attacks Amazon's views
    B. It's ironic
    C. It's unfair
    D. It's sarcastic
    E. It's awkward

28. What is the main conclusion of the author's article?
    A. That Amazon has a lot of market power
    B. That Hachette has a lot of market power
    C. Amazon are disruptive
    D. Amazon has done more for small-time authors than Hachette has done
    E. Amazon's actions against Hachette are just business

29. What did the author imply by the use of the word 'monstrous' in the passage?
    A. That the publishers are monsters
    B. That it's a big task to get a book deal
    C. That it is unacceptably too tough to get a book deal
    D. That authors have to work hard
    E. That authors have to act like monsters

30. Which of the following would, if true, most undermine the author's argument in the final paragraph?
    A. Amazon charge high fees to authors for their 'self-publishing' services
    B. Amazon is not the first company to offer services in self-publishing
    C. Hachette offers the same 'self-publishing' services
    D. Amazon has caused a loss to some authors from their aggressive negotiations with Hachette
    E. Amazon are taking away business from the publishers

31. Which of the following would the author most likely disagree with?
    A. It would be easier for authors to use Amazon's services than that of a traditional publisher
    B. Hachette and Amazon have a lot of market power
    C. Amazon has abused their market position
    D. Hachette has abused their market position
    E. Authors have been given a hard deal by the main publishers

Passage 7 – Online Courts

There are two main ways to resolve a private dispute concerning a question of law. Firstly, you can come to a private settlement with the person you disagree with – this can either (i) just be between the two sides of the case or (ii) involve a third party as a mediator. Alternatively, if that doesn't work, you can sue the other person and seek redress from the courts. It is well known, though, that the court system in the UK is expensive, inefficient, and not suited to the needs of the ordinary person.

Let's say, for example, that you are having an electrician complete some wiring in your house at a price of £300. You pay the electrician and he leaves, but it then transpires that he completed the task erroneously and you want your money back. How do you go about getting it back? Would you go to court? The court fee alone is £35 for each side in the case though and any legal advice from a solicitor would cost approximately £200 per hour. It must be noted that there is a well-established principle that the losing side in a civil case pays the winning side's legal costs. However, in the event that you don't win the case, you could potentially lose even more money from having to pay the winning side's (the electrician's) legal costs.

The cost is disproportionately high here in relation to the value of the claim and herein lies a flaw in the justice system. The high cost limits access to justice. The existing court process takes too long, involves too much paperwork and unnecessarily involves the use of expensive lawyers. Lord Dyson, a leading judge in the Court of Appeal (the second highest court in the UK), echoed these comments. Crucially, there are ways to make the system more efficient and the best way is to introduce an online court.

Firstly, we must accept the truth: lawyers aren't always needed for small-time disputes. We can look to eBay for inspiration. eBay is a well-renowned online auction site where private individuals can sell goods to other individuals. It is not always smooth sailing, however, and frequently disputes arise (for example, when a damaged defective item is sold). When disagreements arise, the seller and buyer are encouraged to negotiate online. If negotiation fails, eBay offers an online resolution service whereby an eBay official decides on the case and makes a binding decision. No lawyers and not even any face-to-face interaction with the eBay official. For simple matters, it would be unnecessary and inefficient to hire a lawyer to complete the task. Crucially, this means much lower costs than in a courtroom.

This system should be used by the justice system for small claims. There should be an online mediation system to allow each side to negotiate in an online discussion area.

Anyone watching the ITV hit television show, 'Judge Rinder', would realise that small-time claims don't require a lawyer. The setting for the show resembles a courtroom where small-time disputes are heard before a 'judge' who mediates between each side. The 'judge' then makes a decision that binds each side. There are no lawyers and each person represents him or herself. While there are a wealth of differences between the TV show and actual court proceedings, it does show that lawyers are not always needed to resolve disputes.

Accordingly, the Government should go one step further and establish an online court to resolve small-time legal disputes. This would involve real judges from the judiciary deciding cases online. They would review the documentary evidence submitted online by the parties and, if necessary, conduct a hearing via video link. While it would cost a lot to set up the online system, it would, in the long run, result in significant cost efficiencies both to the government and to the users of the online court.

32. Which of the following most undermines the author's argument in the second and third paragraphs?
    A. For small claims, people don't need to go to court to resolve disputes – there are alternative methods (such as private mediators)
    B. Such small cases are normally successfully settled outside of court
    C. The UK's justice system is cheaper than that of many other countries in the world
    D. The losing party pays the winning party's legal costs
    E. Solicitors fees for court cases are greater than their fees for out-of-court settlement

33. Assume that you and the plumber go to court. You each take 1 hour of legal advice from a solicitor. How much are the total legal fees for the losing side in the case?
    A. £35
    B. £200
    C. £235
    D. £300
    E. £470

34. Which of the following is an assertion of opinion?
    A. '60 million disagreements between traders and buyers are settled online'
    B. 'the seller and buyer are encouraged to negotiate online'
    C. 'this means much lower costs than in a courtroom'
    D. 'This system should be applied by the justice system'
    E. None of the above

35. Which of the following is implied but not stated about the TV show 'Judge Rinder'?
    A. Judge Rinder decides real cases
    B. The two sides are not represented by lawyers
    C. It is fake
    D. The TV show is not set in a real courtroom
    E. It is innovative

36. Which of the following was not argued by the author?
    A. That an online court should be introduced
    B. The online court should be modelled on the 'Judge Rinder' TV Show
    C. The online court should be modelled on eBay's dispute resolution system
    D. That existing legal costs are too high
    E. Lawyers are not always needed for legal disputes

37. The author argues that the justice system is inefficient. Which of the following best describes why his argument is weak?
    A. It involves a generalisation – the author only referred to small claims but this does not necessarily mean that the whole justice system is inefficient
    B. People don't have to use the justice system to reach a settlement
    C. Only one judge's approval was cited
    D. The author did not say how much the online court would cost
    E. eBay and the justice system are not comparable

Passage 8 – Cars

We live in a world of technological change and it seems that nothing is immune from it. Our phones, computers, kitchens, gardens and cars are all undergoing significant change. If businesses want to keep the custom of consumers, they must engage in technological change and find new, innovative ways to improve their products.

Ever since the introduction of the car over 100 years ago, one thing has remained constant: a human being has always driven the car. While the look, feel, and efficiencies of cars have improved enormously, cars have always required a human being to drive them. Indeed, the law requires human beings to be in control of cars. However, all of this is going to change.

Car companies – and some traditionally non-car companies – have been developing 'driverless cars' at a monumental rate. Famously, TopGear presenter Jeremy Clarkson tried an autonomous BMW around their race track in 2011. While driving on a race track is not comparable to driving on busy roads, there have been significant developments since. Google, for instance, have been testing autonomous cars on open roads in California. A key feature of autonomous vehicles is that they are capable of sensing their environment without human input.

Driverless cars are expected by industry experts to be the norm within 20 years. According to the Society of Motor Manufacturers and Traders, the market for autonomous car technology is expected to contribute £51 billion to the UK economy and over 300,000 jobs. A lot needs to happen in the meantime, though. Car companies need to rigorously test their cars on open roads and the public need to be convinced of their utility. Testing on open roads will allow companies to develop the accuracy and safety of the technology used. Indeed, such testing is essential to develop autonomous cars – how else can we be sure that they will be safe in the real world?

The current law requires a human being to be in control of a car. However, governments have issued special dispensations to car companies wanting to test autonomous cars on public roads. The UK government allow autonomous vehicles to be tested as long as a driver is ready to take over in the case of a system fault. The government has also announced that 40 miles of road in Coventry is to be equipped with technology to aid autonomous vehicles. The significance of the government's support is that it will accelerate the development of autonomous cars and will encourage worldwide car companies to set up permanent research facilities in the UK to test autonomous cars. If the UK can become a world leader in autonomous vehicles, the industry may well contribute a lot more than the expected £50 billion to the UK economy.

However, not everyone is convinced of the success of the driverless car. The CEO of Porsche, a luxury car company, recently dismissed the use of driverless cars, saying that his cars are meant to be driven. That may well be correct for the luxury car market – people want to drive the cars they spend £100,000+ on. However, it does not follow that it's the same for the rest of the car market. People will see that the benefits of autonomous cars outweigh the use of traditional cars. Firstly, autonomous cars are expected to be safer than traditional cars. For instance, a computer system can react much faster than a human to a dangerous situation. Secondly, the driver becomes a passenger and can do something else with his time – the age old saying that time is money still rings true today. This alone will encourage drivers to buy driverless cars. While people may find driverless cars strange initially, they will get used to them. The first desktop computer seemed strange but it is now virtually ubiquitous. So peculiarity should actually be an incentive to development.

38. What is the **main** point the author is making by using the first desktop computer analogy [final paragraph]?
    A. Desktop computers are strange
    B. The public should adapt to the driverless car
    C. People find new things strange
    D. People eventually adapt to new things
    E. The public will adapt to the driverless car

39. What is the underlying **assumption** that the author made in using the first desktop computer analogy?
    A. That people will adapt to new things
    B. People find new things strange
    C. Desktop computers are strange
    D. The public should adapt to the driverless car
    E. Peculiarity should actually be an incentive to development

40. What does the Top Gear autonomous BMW test suggest about the potential for autonomous cars on roads?
    A. It shows that autonomous cars can work on public roads
    B. There would not be accidents from the use of autonomous cars
    C. Autonomous cars will be well received by the public
    D. It would appeal to celebrities, such as Jeremy Clarkson
    E. None of the above

41. What is an underlying theme of the article?
    A. To describe the advent of the driverless car
    B. The autonomous car industry will contribute £50 billion to the UK economy
    C. The public will want to drive an autonomous car
    D. Development of driverless cars has been at a fast rate
    E. There are arguments for and against the adoption of driverless cars

42. Which of the following most undermines the author's argument in the final paragraph?
    A. The fact that driverless cars will be expensive
    B. Cars are meant to be driven
    C. The public would not be convinced by the safety of it
    D. A survey showed that many people are doubtful of the uptake of the autonomous car
    E. The CEO of Porsche is correct

For 367 more LNAT Section A questions check *The Ultimate LNAT Guide*– flick to the back to get a free copy.

SECTION B

The ultimate goal of any essay is to convey an argument to the reader. In order to do that, the essay needs to be as clear as possible, follow a logical structure, and develop a coherent argument. Even though you do not get your mark back from the essay, it is read directly by the admissions tutors at the LNAT Universities you have applied to, which will have a weighting on your application's chances of success.

In the exam, you will have 45 minutes to write the essay.

The key to creating a solid essay in the exam is to develop a good, persuasive argument in clear written English. It is **not** about writing as much as you can – indeed, some of the best essays are the shortest; and a rambling essay can attract low marks.

Ultimately, the examiners are testing your **ability to argue** and **not** particularly on your knowledge. That being said, having a good general knowledge will help you create good arguments and will stand you well for the exam. Crucially, it means that you'll be comfortable answering the questions in the exam.

Structuring your Essay

The structure of an essay consists of 3 parts:

1. Introduction
2. Main Body
3. Conclusion

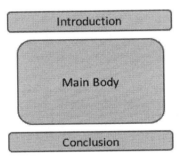

This is a well-known structure and while it is <u>not</u> necessary to give headings or to say that you're writing your introduction, keeping your essay in this format will be more clear and understandable.

A well-known saying is that: in your introduction, say what you're going to say; in the main body, you say it and in your conclusion, say what you've already said by bringing it all together.

The Exam Approach

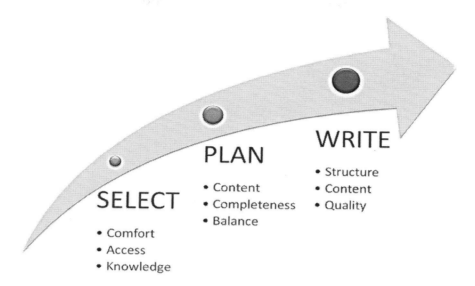

Most students think that the "writing" component is most important. This is simply not true.

The vast **majority of problems are caused by a lack of planning and essay selection** – usually, because students just want to get writing as they are worried about finishing on time. 45 minutes is long enough to be able to plan your essay well and *still* have time to write it, so don't feel pressured to immediately start writing.

Step 1: Selecting

You will be given a choice of 3 essays to choose from and crucially, you will have no idea of what it could be beforehand. Selecting your essay is crucial- make sure you're comfortable with the topic and ensure you understand the actual question- it sounds silly but about 25% of essays that we mark score poorly because they don't actually answer the question!

Take two minutes to read all the questions. Whilst one essay might originally seem the easiest, if you haven't thought through it, you might quickly find yourself running out of ideas. Likewise, a seemingly difficult essay might actually offer you a good opportunity to make interesting points.

Use this time to carefully select which question you will answer by gauging how accessible and comfortable you are with it given your background knowledge.

It's surprisingly easy to change a question into something similar, but with a different meaning. Thus, you may end up answering a completely different essay title. Once you've decided which question you're going to do, read it very carefully a few times to make sure you fully understand it. Answer all aspects of the question. Keep reading it as you answer to ensure you stay on track!

Step 2: Planning

Why should I plan my essay?

There are multiple reasons you should plan your essay for the first 5 minutes of Section B:

- As you don't have much space to write, make the most of it by writing a very well-organised essay.
- It allows you to get all your thoughts ready before you put pen to paper.
- You'll write faster once you have a plan.
- You run the risk of missing the point of the essay or only answering part of it if you don't plan adequately.

How much time should I plan for?

There is no set period of time that should be dedicated to planning, and everyone will dedicate a different length of time to the planning process. You should spend as long planning your essay as you require, but it is essential that you leave enough time to write the essay. As a rough guide, it is **worth spending about 5-10 minutes to plan** and the remaining time on writing the essay. However, this is not a strict rule, and you are advised to tailor your time management to suit your individual style.

How should I go about the planning process?

There are a variety of methods that can be employed in order to plan essays (e.g. bullet-points, mind-maps etc). If you don't already know what works best, it's a good idea to experiment with different methods.

Generally, the first step is to gather ideas relevant to the question, which will form the basic arguments around which the essay is to be built. You can then begin to structure your essay, including the way that points will be linked. At this stage, it is worth considering the balance of your argument, and confirming that you have considered arguments from both sides of the debate. Once this general structure has been established, it is useful to consider any examples or real world information that may help to support your arguments. Finally, you can begin to assess the plan as a whole and establish what your conclusion will be based on your arguments.

How do I plan my essay?

Different methods work best for different students, but some are as follows:

➢ A mind-map
➢ Bullet-points
➢ A side by side list of PROS and CONS

Step 3: Writing

Introduction

The introduction should explain the statement and define any key terms. Here, you can say what you're going to say and suggest (either affirmatively or tentatively) a response or answer to the question.

It is important not to spend too long on an introduction as that would use up too much time unnecessarily, which could be better spent on other parts of the essay.

Main Body

The main body is where you discuss your arguments, consider counter arguments or consider the pros and cons of a particular statement or policy position.

In particular, while you may have numerous ideas, it is generally better to spend more time developing and evaluating fewer points, rather than listing as many points as possible and not going into much depth on each point.

Just like in GCSE English, using the Point-Evidence-Evaluation technique can help ensure you develop and deploy your ideas more fully.

In particular, using relevant examples where you can will help bolster your argument and provide for a more persuasive essay. However, it is crucial that real world examples are only used if they fit in with your argument – otherwise, it adds nothing and will not gain you marks.

How do I go about making a convincing point?
Each idea that you propose should be supported and justified in order to build a convincing overall argument. A point can be solidified through a basic Point → Evidence → Evaluation process. By following this process, you can be assured each sentence within a paragraph builds upon the last and that all the ideas presented are well solidified.

How do I achieve a logical flow between ideas?
One of the most effective ways of displaying a good understanding of the question is to keep a logical flow throughout your essay. This means linking points effectively between paragraphs and creating a congruent train of thought for the examiner as the argument develops. A good way to generate this flow of ideas is to provide ongoing comparisons of arguments and discussing whether points support or dispute one another.

Conclusion

The conclusion provides an opportunity to emphasise the **overall sentiment of your essay** which readers can then take away. It should summarise what has been discussed during the main body and give a definitive answer to the question. It's not necessary to restate your points but this is where you can weigh up the advantages and disadvantages and explain why you've attached more weight to an advantage or disadvantage.

Some students use the conclusion to **introduce a new idea that hasn't been discussed**. This can be an interesting addition to an essay and can help make you stand out. However, it is by no means, a necessity. In fact, a well-organised, 'standard' conclusion is likely to be more effective than an adventurous but poorly executed one.

Crucially, it is important to give a <u>judgement</u> in the conclusion, or a decisive response to the question posed, based on the arguments you've advanced in the main body. For example, do you agree with the statement?

Worked Example

"Abortion should only be permitted in certain circumstances" Discuss.

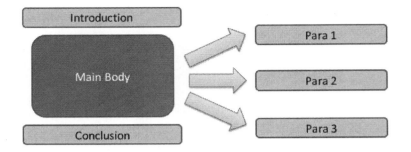

Introduction

In the introduction, it would be useful to present a brief outline of what you're going to discuss. After planning the essay (discussed below), you will know what you're going to talk about in the main body and can give a <u>very brief</u> outline in the introduction.

It is also important to define any key terms in the question here. It is quite clear that 'abortion' could be usefully defined ('the termination of a pregnancy').

If you wish, you can also highlight the key themes that will run through the essay.

Main Body

A key issue is what you write in the main body.

In the planning stage, jot down the ideas that first come to your head. For this question, you should think of possible circumstances where abortion should be permitted and possible circumstances in which it shouldn't be permitted.

Possible circumstances to consider abortion:

➢ *When the mother just wants to give up the foetus*
➢ *In the event of a medical issue*
➢ *Disability of the child*
➢ *Sexual Assault*
➢ *When the mother is too young*

Five possible lines of inquiry are listed here but there won't be time in 40 minutes to consider all of them in enough detail. In the exam, it's much better to focus on <u>quality</u> rather than quantity. Accordingly, choose the areas where you have the most knowledge or where you feel like you can make an original contribution and shine.

It is then necessary to choose a structure, and one possible structure is to devote each paragraph to a 'circumstance' and in order to cover fewer points, but in more detail, three circumstances will be considered. In each paragraph, the pros and cons should be considered to produce a balanced essay.

Structure of Main Body:
1. *Paragraph 1: Abortion when the mother wants to give up foetus*
2. *Paragraph 2: Disability of the child*
3. *Paragraph 3: Medical issue*

Detailed Plan of Main Body

Abortion when the mother wants to give up foetus
For Allowing Abortion:
1. Some may argue that the mother should be able to give up the foetus should she want to.
2. This is based on her freedom to plan her life as she chooses.
3. Forcing the mother to have a child may not be in the child's best interests –would they be cared for?

Against Allowing Abortion
4. The foetus has a right to life.
5. The mother already made her choice during consummation and exercised her freedom to choose then.
6. Therefore, abortion should not be permitted in this circumstance as the right to life should take greater precedence. The mother should be encouraged to think carefully about having a child before consummation.

Disability of the Child
For Allowing Abortion:
7. The child would have a poor quality of life.
8. Would be more expensive to bring up a child with a disability.

Against Allowing Abortion
9. Again, against the child's right to life.
10. Hard to tell what the child's quality of life would be if there's a known disability.
11. Even if the child will be disabled, disabled people play an important role in society.
12. The rights of a foetus shouldn't be different depending on a disability.
13. Arguably, the right to life of the foetus should prevail here. It would, in any case, be discriminatory to lower the rights of an abnormal foetus when compared to that of a healthy foetus. It's against the law to discriminate against disabled humans and surely the same should be the case for a disabled foetus.

Medical Issue
For Allowing Abortion
14. Health risk to the mother.
Against Allowing Abortion
15. Right to life of the foetus.
16. On balance, the right to life of a living person should take precedence in this circumstance.

This is a detailed plan and your plan in the exam does not need to be this detailed, but it should still cover the main points. Once a plan is written, you can get straight into writing the essay.

Note carefully how alternative points of view are <u>always</u> considered in the detailed plan above. Ultimately, your goal is to write a persuasive and balanced essay. When you consider alternative points of view, it strengthens your main argument. This is because it shows that you have thought about the different sides of the issue.

In the detailed plan above, point (c) is an intermediate (or interim) conclusion at the end of each paragraph. This is simply a statement which concludes a *paragraph*. It is generally desirable to include tentative conclusions where possible here as it makes it easier for the reader to understand your essay.

Conclusion

In the conclusion, the arguments advanced in the main body are brought together. In this question, the interim conclusions on each circumstance went into a lot of depth, so just a basic summary suffices for the main conclusion. An example could be as follows:

"On balance, abortion should only be permitted in certain circumstances. The right to life of the foetus demands that abortion is not allowed at the behest of the mother alone. However, there are certain situations when abortion should be permitted, such as when there is a health risk to the mother as her rights must be considered alongside that of the foetus."

Common Mistakes

1) Ignoring the other side of the argument

Although you're normally required to support one side of the debate, it is important to **consider arguments against your judgement** in order to get the higher marks. A good way to do this is to propose an argument that might be used against you, and then to argue why it doesn't hold true or seem relevant. You may use the format: *"some may say that...but this doesn't seem to be important because..."* in order to dispel opposition arguments whilst still displaying that you have considered them. For example, *"some may say that fox hunting shouldn't be banned because it is a tradition. However, witch hunting was also once a tradition – we must move on with the times"*.

2) Answering the topic/Answering only part of the question

One of the most common mistakes is to only answer a part of the question whilst ignoring the rest of it as it's inaccessible.

3) Long Introductions

Some students can start rambling and make introductions too long and unfocused. Although background information about the topic can be useful, it is normally not necessary. Instead, the **emphasis should be placed on responding to the question**. Some students also just **rephrase the question** rather than actually explaining it. The examiner knows what the question is, and repeating it in the introduction is simply a waste of space.

4) Not including a Conclusion

An essay that lacks a conclusion is incomplete and can signal that the answer has not been considered carefully or that your organisation skills are lacking. **The conclusion should be a distinct paragraph** in its own right and not just a couple of rushed lines at the end of the essay.

5) Sitting on the Fence

Students sometimes don't reach a clear conclusion. You need to **ensure that you give a decisive answer to the question** and clearly explain how you've reached this judgement. Essays that do not come to a clear conclusion generally have a smaller impact and score lower.

General Advice

- ✓ Always answer the question clearly – this is the key thing examiners look for in an essay.
- ✓ Analyse each argument made, justifying or dismissing with logical reasoning.
- ✓ Keep an eye on the time/space available – an incomplete essay may be taken as a sign of a candidate with poor organisational skills.
- ✓ Use pre-existing knowledge when possible – examples and real world data can be a great way to strengthen an argument- but don't make up statistics!
- ✓ Present ideas in a neat, logical fashion (easier for an examiner to absorb).
- ✓ Complete some practice papers in advance in order to best establish your personal approach to the paper (particularly timings, how you plan etc.).
- ✓ Attempt to answer a question that you don't fully understand, or ignore part of a question.
- ✓ Rush or attempt to use too many arguments – it is much better to have fewer, more substantial points.
- ✓ Attempt to be too clever or present false knowledge to support an argument – a tutor may call out incorrect facts etc.
- ✓ Panic if you don't know the answer the examiner wants – there is no right answer, the essay is not a test of knowledge but a chance to display reasoning skill.
- ✓ Leave an essay unfinished – if time/space is short, wrap up the essay early in order to provide a conclusive response to the question.

ANNOTATED ESSAYS

Example Essay 1

"There is a time and place for censorship of the internet" Discuss with particular reference to the right of freedom of expression.

Internet is the main source of connection for people all around the world. It's where we get the latest news and information worldwide effectively and effortlessly. The lack of barrier in this internet world gives easy access to information that we might not want to see and might cause us offence. This essay is about the act of censorship, which filters offensive information of the internet, given there's a time and a place we can do so in this modern era. There's "a place" suggests there's enough room which needs to be censored and there's "a time" suggest it's the time to act on censorship.

Firstly, censorship is necessary to a certain extent as due to freedom of expression, we might be access to information that we found offended by, such as pornography. These might affect viewers mentally and easily cause depression, and affect minds especially the early teens.
However, an age limit could be set on a pornography website and refuse access to such images. It's taking an active role, to click into those websites. Setting age limits can prevent youngsters receiving non-educational information and affect their youth development. Freedom of expression is also offended as some might treat pornography as a form of art. It's very difficult to monitor whether the viewer is really above the age limit.

Also, definition of Art is very blurry, which as an excuse for people to share it through the internet. Parental education is also a key. Instead of setting limits to the children, we should given them advice on what they should go on, and guide them to make the right decision on choosing suitable materials. In this way, not only the children's development is protected, it also trains them to give the right judgements and develop logical thinking.

Another place for censorship is political/religious offensive comments and materials. Religious behaviours should be protected due to the freedom of expression in society and political views in order to keep harmony. However, in order to achieve this, censorship is not necessary, as it would block the minds and thoughts and might be a chance for the government to brain-wash the citizens with the 'right kind' of political behaviour, which might ironically break harmony in society, and slow down its development.

Examiner's Comments:

Introduction: The introduction rambles on too long – it could have been much shorter and concise. It was also not clear. It's not necessary to say "This essay is about the act of censorship" – this is obvious. It was good to define censorship in the introduction (when the student said 'filters offensive information') although the rest of the introduction was not clear and did not make sense. Accordingly, the student would have lost marks here and wasted time. The student did not address the entire question either – it would have been good to point out how freedom of expression will come into play as well. The introduction only really needs to be 3 or 4 lines.

Main Body: In the main body, the student makes some wild assertions, such as the point regarding depression. The first sentence in the main body doesn't make much sense either. The main issue with the essay is that the student's points are not linked together logically: the essay consists of a large number of separate assertions. The point made about 'art' is not very clear either.

Conclusion: Lastly, the candidate finishes with no conclusion. The final paragraph did not draw together all the relevant information, which is bad practice. Even if a candidate is running out of time, writing a solid conclusion will gain many more marks than not writing one. Indeed, a lack of conclusion would likely lose marks.

Example Essay 2

"There is a time and place for censorship of the internet" Discuss with particular reference to the right of freedom of expression.

Censorship of the internet is not a new concept, nor does it seem like one that will ever cease. I believe that there are a multitude of reasons for its presence and hence in this essay I will argue for the statement provided.

Firstly, censorship of the internet has the capability to protect certain groups. For example, a widely accepted and often promoted form of this is the blocking of certain websites by parents and schools. In this case, the group being protected are children. We accept the fact that children should not be exposed to 'mature' content such as violence and sexual activity and by blocking certain sites, children are free to surf the internet safely. This seemingly innocent form of censorship hardly poses much threat to the right to freedom of expression as no party is being prevented from having their views heard. If this form of censorship was deemed illegal, it may paradoxically push such parties to tone down their content by pressures from parental organisations and child safety bodies in order to create a child friendly internet, which ultimately would be restrictive to free expression.

Secondly, the restriction of content that is deemed extremist or might incite acts of terrorism, whilst going against the right to freedom of expression, could be necessary to uphold the security of a nation. Thus, taking a utilitarian perspective to this issue, as the safety of the nation takes on a greater value than the right to freedom of expression. Although it may seem like a cold approach, it is justified for the well-being of a greater number of individuals and thus, society generally. Truly, the recruitment of ISIS supports is a disturbing example of the necessity of censorship of extremist views and preventative measures must be taken to ensure that the young and susceptible are not taken in by the terrorist propaganda. Accordingly, there must be a point where we deem the safety of a nation as more imperative than the freedom of expression of certain individuals.

Lastly, the freedom of expression is easily abused in the cyber world. The animosity that the internet provides gives the users a sense of invisibility where they see themselves as above the law. Abusive remarks are made without consideration of their consequence or lack of this providing an environment for cyber bullying to grow.

Censorship is not necessarily tyrannical but is a practice that must co-exist with any form of content creation and like all else, there is a time and place for it.

Examiner's Comments:
Introduction: The introduction is very concise, which is good. However, it would have been even better if the student considered freedom of expression in the introduction.

Main Body: This is a good attempt at the question and relates directly to the question. The candidate refers to the relationship between censorship and freedom of expression throughout the main body. She points out when freedom of expression is hindered by censorship and when censorship is justified. Given that it relates to the question throughout, it would yield many more marks than Example 1 (even though both are of a similar length).

However, the candidate did not consider whether censorship might be bad in the first place: why can't the government just censor what they want to? The essay would have been stronger if this were considered (even briefly). It would have been worthwhile to bring in the countervailing principle of 'freedom of expression' at some point in the essay. This would be a reason why the government should *not* be able to censor any information. The penultimate paragraph doesn't add much to the essay though – is censorship acceptable in this situation? Is this the place for censorship? Or should people be expected to put up with other people's views? Other than this paragraph, the rest of the essay is very good.

Conclusion: The conclusion is quite short. While there is nothing inherently wrong with the conclusion being concise, it must answer the question. The candidate's conclusion did not refer to freedom of expression and so she has not fully addressed the question.

Example Essay 3

"There is a time and place for censorship of the internet" Discuss with particular reference to the right of freedom of expression".

In today's day and age it's extremely easy for anyone to access explicit or dangerous content on the internet. There have been talks of censorship on the internet, but is it necessary? One would argue that the censorship of the internet is against our freedom of expression, which is why in this essay I will come with an answer in response to the statement 'There is a time and place for censorship of the internet'.

In our current education system there is a heavy emphasis put on the usage of the internet to aid our learning. However, once children learn how to use the internet, the whole world is just one click away. Children could be easily exposed to indecent images, which is why some say the government should censor the internet for the safety of children. Possible solutions could be only allowing websites with adult material to be accessible at late-night, reducing the chances of indecent exposure to children. Accordingly, in this instance, censorship is justified.

Similarly, one could easily research the internet to find information about illegal activities such as drug or bomb making. This means that the internet could be used as a tool to threaten national security, hence why the internet should have tough censorship in order to prevent criminals from accessing dangerous material, for the benefit of everyone's safety.

On the other hand, blocking certain websites strictly goes against our right of freedom of expression and instead of blocking certain dangerous websites, the government should have a more efficient surveillance strategy in order to track people who are accessing such dangerous websites. This would ensure that our right of freedom of expression isn't breached and at the same time, criminal activity would be prevented.

Furthermore, with regards to the access of sexually explicit websites, more work should be some in order to educate children not to access such websites. Good parent is a better alternative to preventing children accessing such websites, rather than blocking sites which goes against our right of freedom of expression.

In conclusion, there is no time and place for censorship as it goes against our right to freedom of expression. Other alternatives such as internet surveillance would be more effective as it ensures the safety of the general public and at the same time our freedom of expression is not breached.

Examiner's Comments:

Introduction: This is a very good introduction. It highlights the conflict between censorship and freedom of expression, which is a good place to point it out. In the final sentence, though, the student wastes time in saying "which is why in this essay I will come with an answer in response to the statement...." – this is obvious and there's little point in saying it. It just wastes time and prevents one using the time for writing something more useful. Other than this, the introduction is very good and concise.

Main Body: The student considers two main instances of censorship in the main body (indecent images and dangerous websites) and suggests that censorship could be used, but suggests alternatives would be more effective. This is quite a persuasive essay because the student has considered alternative points of view, which makes the essay balanced.

Conclusion: The conclusion is very clear and brings the arguments advanced in the essay to a final judgement. The candidate directly addresses the question and refers to the whole part of the question by considering freedom of expression (unlike in Example Essay 2). On the whole, this is a very impressive essay.

Example Essay 4

"The UK should codify its Constitution" Discuss.

The present constitution of the UK includes sources such as statute law and case law made by the judges. To codify the constitution, the state should come up with one single document that explains and describes the power of the Royal family, the government, the parliament and all the citizens. This essay will critically examine the possibility of codifying the UK's constitution.

Firstly, a codified constitution can make it clear and accessible to the citizens. With a written constitution, the citizens can trace back the rights and obligations of them and also have a better understanding of the relationship between them and the government. This may motivate the UK people to be active in partaking in politics because they can feel that they have a say through voting or other political actions.

Secondly, it helps limit the power of the government. Since the government is formed by the winning party of the election of the House of Commons, the party which is in charge of the government has the strength to implement the policies that they are fond of, even if it opposes the public will. A written constitution which clarifies the duty and the power of a government that when the government does not go in accordance with the public opinion, the constitution will help prevent it from doing so.

However, it is actually unique that the parliament is supreme of all. The parliament should have the ability to change the law or add new rules according to the demand of the public, neither any other organisations nor rules should have a bigger say than parliament, which is elected by the people. If the Constitution is codified, there will be a constitutional court like USA does with judges who are not elected to interpret the law. It actually weakens our democracy.

Furthermore, an uncodified constitution is more flexible. For the UK, getting enough support and votes in the Parliament is the only factor to change the content of a law or add a new act. It only takes a minimal period of time to adopt a new policy which benefits the country. This is totally opposite to the rigid process of changing regulations and rules in a country with a codified constitution such as France, which takes a very long time to pass through all stages to get consent from difference levels. A flexible system helps a country react to international changes faster and diminishes the losses it can possibly come up with.

In addition, the UK does not have a revolution in history to set up the Constitution. Unlike other countries with written constitutions, the UK did not have any revolution (such as in France and the US) to overthrow the old system and set up a democracy. It gradually changes from authoritarian rule of monarch to a state with constitutional monarch. The past has shown that the country actually works well with this system while the democracy of the country does not disappear. It always ranks top 10 in the world, a place where many developing countries would like to learn.

To conclude, it is unnecessary for the UK to set up a codified constitution because the existing system alas makes the country work well. No one can ensure what effects the written one will bring to the UK.

Examiner's Comments:

This is a relatively long essay for 45 minutes, but one which is not that good. It uses a lot of knowledge, but not to good effect.

Introduction: This is concise in just explaining the role of a codified constitution. The issue is that it does not define what a codified constitution is. Having a written constitution is more than just having the constitution written in a single document: It is one which is harder to repeal than other laws.

This is not a big concern to the essay though as the Section B essay is more a test of your persuasive and written skills, rather than your essay. It would also be worth pointing out that an unwritten constitution (like the UK's) is flexible, which means that a government can just change it if it wants. Whereas a written constitution (like in the US) binds the government and Parliament and a special majority is required to alter it. Highlighting such policy tensions can be beneficial in the introduction to essay questions.

Main Body:

Everything you say in the essay must make sense. It is pointless writing the first thing which comes to your mind if it doesn't make sense as this would paint a poor picture with admissions tutors and lead to rejection. In the second paragraph, it is not clear how the sentence "*This may motivate the UK people to be active in partaking in politics because they can feel that they have a say through voting or other political actions*" relates to the question. It isn't clear that people feel they can have a say through voting by virtue of having a written constitution, and the student does not explain it. The sentence does not actually make sense.

The third paragraph is not entirely clear either – surely a government would reflect the public will. It would be more coherent to suggest that the government can infringe on minority rights.

At the beginning of the fourth paragraph, the candidate starts with the sentence: "*However, it is actually unique that the parliament is supreme of all.*" This particular point is not elaborated on further and it does not add to the essay. So what if Britain's system is unique? Does this mean it's bad? It is important to be clear in essays, to make the reader's job (of understanding what you mean) as easy as possible. The candidate also incorrectly uses the connective 'However' – this connection is used to indicate a contrasting point but the student's points before and after the connective do not contrast! This goes to show that it is important to think before writing and ensure you express yourself clearly.

The candidate has clearly deployed significant knowledge but has not used it well to advance an argument and the essay has been confusing at many points. It is important to think and plan what you're going to write before writing it; planning before writing can significantly help the quality of writing. This essay would have likely led to rejections by admissions tutors.

A crucial suggestion would be to think whether you are addressing the question while answering it.

Conclusion: The conclusion is sufficient as it directly answers the question.

Example Essay 5

"The UK should codify its Constitution" Discuss.

Currently, the UK has an uncodified constitution. This means that there is no single legal document defining and storing all of the laws and regulations in the UK. The UK constitution comprises of many different areas. The ambiguity of the UK constitution has created debate within government itself as well as outside of government.

One main reason as to why the constitution should be codified is due to it being ambiguous. Certain laws become ignored as it may be presumed not legislative despite it being a tradition, or an 'unproven rule'. Theresa May, the Home Secretary, violated one of the constitutional conventions, where she publicly blamed and identified one of the civil servants for a mishap in passport checking in Paris. It is known in government that the head of authority is to take responsibility of everything, whether it is or not their fault. Due to there not being a codified constitution, Theresa May was able slip from it. Therefore, having a codified constitution can ensure full responsibility to government.

Furthermore, a codified constitution provides security to the citizens, they would know that government is bounded by a tight set of rules which has little of no loopholes and can easily be accountable for any mistakes. This reduces confusion among the public as well, as there is a clear definition between right and wrong. A legal and authoritative constitution disregards any form of unfair or unequal treatment within the hierarchy.

However, looking at it from a different perspective, the constitution has been within the UK for a long time and has been fine with no major problems. Codifying the constitution may stir major changes and cause unpopularity among those in power. So if it isn't broken, why change it? The constitution's long standing in the UK and is also a form of historical standing which has become an admiration of many countries. It also symbolises trust in government by the people. The constitution holds more than just rights and rules, but also a devoting history in the country. As long as it has been here, there have been no issues with it.

In addition, an uncodified constitution is said to be flexible and up to date. This is because it can easily be changed and corrected if flawed. The bills of rights in the US takes a lengthy and long process to be altered. However, in the UK, adding or removing the law requires not a great amount of time. The flexibility of the constitution is a greatly appreciated characteristic of it, making it unique.

In conclusion, the constitution is fine as it is and does not require change. It is the government's own responsibility to maintain professionalism within parliament and not the laws. There is still the stance of democracy among the people to hold those of government accountable if there is any distasteful occurrence.

Examiner's Comments:

Introduction: The introduction started on the right approach, which was to explain what is meant by a codified constitution. However, the student gave an incorrect definition. It's not correct that all of a country's laws would be in a constitution.

Main Body: Each of the middle four paragraphs in the main body discuss interesting and relevant points in a lucid and concise way. The candidate presents arguments for and then arguments against, then comes to a final conclusion. To improve the essay, it would have been worth trying to evaluate and weigh up the pros and cons a bit more. For example, considering the final point in the fifth paragraph more would have been better – such as, "the flexibility has received criticisms for governments being able to make significant constitutional change, but it has crucially allowed the UK's constitution to adapt to changes in society, which may not have otherwise been possible". A further relevant point would be that the Human Rights Act may help reach a balance.

Conclusion: The first sentence is fine. It is not clear how the rest of the paragraph addresses the question. It would have been clearer if the candidate said: "The government is more accountable under an un-codified constitution".

For 10 more Section B example essays check the *Ultimate LNAT Guide*– flick to the back to get a free copy.

WORKED ANSWERS

LNAT Section A

Q	A	Q	A	Q	A	Q	A
1	B	11	B	21	D	31	C
2	B	12	E	22	C	32	B
3	E	13	C	23	D	33	E
4	C	14	A	24	D	34	D
5	A	15	C	25	B	35	D
6	D	16	A	26	B	36	B
7	A	17	C	27	B	37	A
8	D	18	C	28	E	38	E
9	C	19	E	29	C	39	A
10	E	20	C	30	C	40	E
						41	A
						42	C

Passage 1

Question 1: B
The opponents said that drug consumption is criminogenic because a drug addiction 'can lead to other crimes'. Option A is incorrect as the passage already states that consuming drugs is in itself a criminal offence. Thus, it would be odd and circular if opponents were to argue this.

Question 2: B
It is close between A and B. In regard to A, the author merely points out a 'contrast', which may not necessarily indicate an inconsistency, whereas the author says, in the context of option B in the passage that there is 'incoherence', which clearly means there is an inconsistency. Therefore, the author *presented* B as being paradoxical.

Question 3: E
The entire article is based on the idea of controlled drugs being legalised. Each sub-argument provides an intermediate conclusion from which the main argument is inferred.

Question 4: C
The author does not argue that drug consumption would fall (as distinct from highlighting that it fell for one age group in Portugal) or increase, so A and B are incorrect. The author implied that drug consumption should be seen as a *present* public health problem in the passage – not that it would be a health concern once drugs were legalised so E is wrong. D is not a practical effect which the author believes would happen. C is explicitly stated in the passage.

Question 5: A
The author has based his argument on the fact that there aren't third party effects to taking drugs (e.g. no third party health effects & that the fact of criminalising increases secondary offences). However, if drug consumption increases one's propensity for violence, it contradicts that argument.

Passage 2

Question 6: D

The passage attacks a generalisation and shows an example that refutes one given to the 'musical' genre. Nothing is mentioned of Sondheim's talents, or what his role was in creating the musical, nor are there claims made in relation to Wheeler's literary tastes (he may just like ONE penny dreadful). This musical may deal with morbid themes, but that's not to say that most do - it could be only a select few that do.

Question 7: A

The pies make the crimes 'culinary' in nature, the mention of revenge shows Todd's illegal acts to be 'vengeful', the word 'macabre' indicates it's disturbing and the judge's rape is a 'sexual' crime. There is nothing explicitly suggesting the crimes of any party are funny, or to be considered funny.

Question 8: D

This option is essentially synonymous in the quoted belief, 'we all deserve to die', which includes both bad and good people and makes no significant reference to gender exclusion/inclusion.

Question 9: C

There are four mentioned themes, but that does not mean there are only four themes, nor does 'legal corruption' get named as the central theme. As the entirety of Sweeney Todd is not discussed in the passage, only a central plot line, one could not exclude the potential of something positive happening in the play - even a minor incident. Sadness in itself, therefore, cannot be considered the focus of the play. The themes mentioned are, however, indeed macabre.

Question 10: E

Though the original title 'A String of Pearls: A Romance' may appear to suggest a romantic relationship within the narrative, nothing in the passage states the two are a couple so A is incorrect. The passage only suggested that *some* of the songs were removed, not all of the songs, so B is incorrect. We can't be sure about D as the passage does not refer to the critical acclaim of the film. In regard to C, while some changes were made to the film, we aren't told whether the main storyline changes. Finally, E is explicitly stated in the passage, so that must be true.

Passage 3

Question 11: B

This is mentioned as an impact on the country in the passage and not mentioned as having a personal impact, whereas all others are mentioned as personal impacts. Also, as is evident from the term itself, an increase in government spending affects the government. The focus of the point was on the government's spending (rather than on any welfare benefits derived).

Question 12: E

This option is explicitly stated in the passage.

Question 13: C

This is implied as the author states the numerous benefits of high-quality education provision but also notes how 'more emphasis' should be placed on it. Crucially, it says that vocational education is 'second rate' and that it must change. A clear implication of these sentences is that more should be done to encourage vocational courses. E is already stated in the passage (as the author highlights the negative consequences). The author also explicitly states A, B, and D. Therefore, since they are all stated in the passage, they are incorrect.

Question 14: A

While the author does argue for B, it is only part of the main argument and is in the context of increasing high-quality vocational provision for young people. The skills shortage was used more as a reason to argue for A. Given the emphasis on raising vocational education, it is clear that A is the correct answer. The author does not argue for C and actually points out that the jobs are already there, it's just that young people need to be trained more. D was not argued for and E was an assertion (and, thus, not an argument, let alone a main argument).

Question 15: C

This is explicitly stated in the passage. A is not stated in the passage. While Dulux was increasing young people's skills, the author did not advocate this for businesses generally and, thus, B is incorrect. The author suggested that D and E should be done by the government, rather than by businesses.

Passage 4

Question 16: A

B, C, and D are all stated as influences in the passage but option A is stated as underlying all those reasons and thus, A is the 'ultimate' influence.

Question 17: C

The passage mentions that a son was required to secure the Tudor dynasty. Therefore, there is something familial relating to all of this. Therefore, B and E are incorrect. D doesn't follow from the sentence so it has to be either A or C. A doesn't make sense in this context as it's not clear how having a son would secure his family but C fits in well.

Question 18: C

Royal Supremacy was merely the process of getting control over the church and was not a reason for getting a son (it was the means to getting the son) so A is wrong. B is incorrect as it should be the other way round – he wanted to divorce Catherine to get a son (and not get a son to divorce Catherine). C fits in with the passage and, thus, is correct.

Question 19: E

A and D were stated in the passage, so are incorrect. Even if B and C were true, they would not weaken any of the conclusions, so they are not correct. However, E is correct as if he believed that he could get a divorce from Rome, he would have tried to get that as it was the 'straightforward' option. The author also stated that without Henry's desire for a break from Rome, it wouldn't have happened. Therefore, point E would be a necessary assumption to support the author's points.

Question 20: C

The passage never suggests that the Act of Supremacy is the royal supremacy, so E is incorrect. The passage states that the Royal Supremacy was established once Henry became the only head of the church, so C is, thus, correct as it means the King had become the leader of the church. D is, therefore, obviously incorrect as the Pope isn't the head of the English church. B is too vague and while option A had to occur for the Royal Supremacy to take place, the passage pointed out that C was, in fact, the royal supremacy.

Passage 5

Question 21: D

The passage explicitly states that charities may not need to pay corporation tax. A is not true based on the passage – as you can provide a public benefit but have not registered to be a charity. It is only after registration as a charity that an institution gets the fiscal benefits; this does not happen automatically. B and C are not proved in the passage, and E is an opinion, which can't be true or false. In regard to C specifically, it cannot be assumed that just because event X is required for event Y to occur that if Y does not occur, X does not occur – in the context of the passage, you can still provide a public benefit and not be a charity. Therefore, C is incorrect.

Question 22: C

The passage explicitly states that it's "necessary" for an institution to demonstrate that its purposes are for the public benefit.

Question 23: D

Both C and E are easily eliminated as neither of these institutions were part of the trial, which is where the argument was advanced. We're told that tribunal judges didn't consider the argument and it is, thus, clear by implication that they didn't bring it forward (therefore, B is incorrect), so we're left with either A or D. It's not A as the argument weakens their position (being independent schools) so it's unlikely they would advance it. By elimination, therefore, it must be the Education Review Group, D.

Question 24: D

Whether the law should or should not allow a free-for-all is not a point that can be tested – it is a person's opinion and cannot be true or false. All the other options can be tested.

Question 25: B

In the passage, it is stated that the tribunal said that children who couldn't afford the fees of private schools must benefit from them for there to be a 'public benefit'. Accordingly, providing scholarships to others who can't afford the fees would help with this. A is insufficient to meet the tribunal's definition. C, D, and E do not support the argument that there's a public benefit.

Passage 6

Question 26: B

Amazon is more powerful. The author said that one is more powerful than the other at the beginning of the passage and it later becomes clear that Amazon is more powerful as they were able to restrict the sales of Hatchette's books in negotiations, thus, indicating a stronger bargaining position.

Question 27: B

There is irony because Hatchette have done aggressive things, just like Amazon have and yet, they are now complaining about Amazon.

Question 28: E

This option draws all of the points expressed in the passage together. Even though Amazon engaged in aggressive tactics, others have done it too and Amazon have done beneficial things. It gets to the heart of the passage, which is considering the actions of Amazon.

Question 29: C

The word 'monstrous' implies not only that there is a big task, but that the task is too big as the word implies some dissatisfaction with all the work that authors have to do.

Question 30: C

If Hachette had offered the same services as Amazon had, it would directly contradict what the author has said – Amazon's services wouldn't be an 'innovation', Hachette (one of the 'big publishers') would not have been acting unfairly in the past and Hachette would have been acting to the benefit of small authors: this would all be contrary to the author's points in the final paragraph; therefore, point C most undermines the author's argument.

Question 31: C

The author has been positive about what Amazon has done throughout the article. Therefore, the author would most likely disagree with the suggestion that Amazon has abused their market position. The author has acknowledged A, B, and E in the article. The author isn't likely to agree with D because Hachette had engaged in a conspiracy.

Passage 7

Question 32: B

The answer here is between A and B, both undermine the author's argument that the court system limits access to justice. B *most* undermines the author's argument because if these cases are normally settled out of court, the court system's high cost does not limit access to justice as people would already be getting justice, albeit outside the court system. Option A doesn't undermine it as much because it just says that there are different options for small claimants, whereas B directly cuts at the option. C, D, and E don't necessarily undermine the author's argument.

Question 33: E

This question necessitates being able to deduce the correct information from the passage and shows whether you've understood the passage. 1 hour of legal advice is £200 and the court fee for each is £35. Therefore, the cost for each side is £235. Therefore, the cost for both sides together is £470. As the passage stated that the losing side pays the winning side's costs (as well as their own), the losing side would have to pay a total of £470. N.B. there have been similar questions to this in recent LNATs.

Question 34: D

This is a statement that cannot be tested as true or false and is a normative statement. Therefore, it is an opinion.

Question 35: D

A and B are true but they are explicitly stated in the passage, so are incorrect (the question explicitly asks for an option which is *not stated*). Neither C nor E can be implied. The passage states that the TV show 'resembles' a courtroom, thereby implying that it is not actually a real courtroom but some kind of mock courtroom that looks similar.

Question 36: B

Despite discussing the Judge Rinder show, the author never advances an argument that an online court should be modelled on it – just that the TV show shows that lawyers aren't needed.

Question 37: A

B doesn't even relate to whether the justice system is inefficient or not, so that's incorrect. Again, D and E don't relate to whether the *current* justice system is efficient. On the other hand, option A points out that the author has only referred to a subset of claims (i.e. small claims) and not considered the justice system generally. In particular, no reference was made to the criminal justice system. It doesn't follow that just because one part of it is inefficient, that the rest of it is inefficient. Therefore, A is correct as it highlights why that argument was weak.

Passage 8

Question 38: E

The author made the analogy in order to demonstrate that even though the driverless car may seem strange, people will still adapt to it. Therefore, E is correct. A is wrong as the author only says that at the first part of the analogy. C doesn't necessarily follow. While D is, in essence, what the author is saying, he's applied it to driverless cars. Therefore, his *main* point is that the public will adapt to the driverless car. Since the author was not arguing that the public *should* take up the driverless car with the analogy, B is incorrect.

Question 39: A

The assumption made is that people adapt to new things.

Question 40: E

The Top Gear test doesn't suggest any of A, B, C or D in respect of the use of autonomous cars *on roads*. A, B, C are obviously not demonstrated by the passage. D is not relevant to the question and would be a generalisation as well.

Question 41: A

Throughout, the author describes different aspects of the take-up of driverless cars by car companies and governments and only considers the benefits of it to drivers in the final paragraph. The author does not point out arguments for and against, so E is incorrect. Indeed, the author's view is that the public will want to drive such a car, but this does not underlie the entire piece, so C is incorrect. The same is true with option B. Again, while D is true, it is not the underlying theme of the article.

Question 42: C

E is incorrect as it doesn't relate to the author's main argument in the final paragraph – indeed, the author even acknowledged point E in respect of luxury cars. In regard to B and D, which relate to how cars are currently (B) or the current views on it (D), the author argues that there will be an uptake of it *in the future*. B and D just relate to the present and, thus, don't undermine the author's argument. If C were true, though, this would undermine the author's argument as the public may not take it up in that case. A doesn't necessarily show that people won't take up driverless cars. Therefore, A is incorrect.

END OF SECTION

THE CAMBRIDGE LAW TEST

The Basics

What is the CLT?

The Cambridge Law Test (CLT) is a one-hour written exam for law students who are applying to the University of Cambridge. You have one hour to answer an essay-based question, and you are not expected to have any pre-requisite knowledge of the law. You will be assessed based on your clarity of expression and how you interpret a particular essay question. The test is used as a further piece of information to assess a candidate's suitability for admission into Cambridge.

Test Structure

You will be given a choice from three essay questions, from which you only have to do one. It is a paper-based test, unless you have special circumstances. The test structure might differ if you are doing your interview overseas.

Who has to sit the CLT?

Only candidates who have been shortlisted for the Cambridge Law Interview will be asked to sit for the test. It is generally done before your interview, subject to differences depending on which college you have applied for.

Why is the CLT used?

The CLT was developed by University of Cambridge as an alternative to the LNAT in order for them to assess a candidate's suitability for reading law in Cambridge. Hence, students applying to read law in University of Cambridge will not need to sit the LNAT. The CLT differs from the LNAT as the CLT does not comprise a multiple choice questions (MCQ) section. Candidates are only expected to write one essay question within an hour, and the essays tend to skew more towards legal questions as opposed to general current affairs essay questions that the LNAT tends to cover.

When do I sit the CLT?

You will be informed by the college you have applied to whether you are shortlisted for the interview, and if you are they will arrange your CLT accordingly, which is likely to take place before your interview when you have arrived in Cambridge for your interview. If you have applied for an interview overseas, separate arrangements will be made and your college will inform you of the relevant dates and venue.

How much does it cost?

Taking the CLT is completely free; the college will arrange the test for you if you are shortlisted for interview.

Can I re-sit the CLT?

You will not be allowed to re-sit the CLT, but if you are unsuccessful following the interview you can request for feedback to gauge how well you did in the CLT, and this might help you should you wish to re-apply to Cambridge the following year.

If I re-apply, do I have to resit the CLT?

As mentioned above, if you re-apply to Cambridge, you will be asked to sit the CLT again.

When do I get my results?

If you are successful following the interview, you will generally not find out how well you did for the CLT. However, if you are unsuccessful, you can request feedback from the college which you applied to and they will tell you your score on the CLT.

Where do I sit the CLT?

It will generally be in the college which you will be interviewing in. If you have requested for an overseas interview, separate arrangements will be made and your college will inform you accordingly.

How is the CLT scored?

The essay, similarly to the interview, is scored on a scale of 1-10, 1 being the worst and 10 being the best. Successful candidates will usually score at least a 7 to stand a good chance of being admitted, but do take not that the CLT is just one factor taken into account – the interview, your personal statement, and any extra essays you may be asked to submit all play a part.

How is the CLT used?

The University of Cambridge Faculty of Law website states that the Cambridge Law Test is only intended to complement the other elements of their admissions process, such as the interview, your personal statement, and your grades to date.

How does my score compare?

As mentioned above, successful candidates tend to score at least a 7 on a scale of 10, but this is subject to how well you have done on your interview, how good your grades are, and your personal statement.

Access Arrangements

If you require special circumstances such as extra time or a separate room, you should always arrange this with the college which you will be interviewing in beforehand. The college will contact you if you are shortlisted for interview and ask whether you require any special circumstances.

General Advice

Practice

A good place to start will be to refer to this guide! Whilst it is stated that you do not need any prior knowledge of law to do the CLT, it is good to read up on the fundamental principles of law so you start to think and write like a lawyer, and be able to understand the more legalistic questions that the CLT tends to set. You should also look at our sample essays to differentiate a good essay from a bad one, before having a go at practicing a few essay titles so that you are confident and prepared on the day itself.

Start Early

You should get into the habit of preparing early, and a good way to start is to start a daily habit of reading legal news so that you are exposed to the kind of topics that tend to be asked in the CLT. There are plenty of news websites that provide free legal news, such as the law section of The Guardian and The Telegraph. If you have a subscription to The Financial Times or The Economist, they provide excellent legal news from time to time as well.

How to Work

You should focus on reading as widely as possible about the law so that you will not be stumped by all the questions available to you during the actual test. They can be on very specific topics such as corporate manslaughter or intellectual property law, and once again whilst they do not expect you to have any prior knowledge of law, it helps if you have read up about such issues and have a general idea about the points you can raise and how to structure your essay in a succinct and cohesive manner. You should also practice writing essays under timed conditions so that you are able to produce a sufficiently detailed essay within one hours setting out all the key points you can make regarding a particular essay question.

Focus on topics you are comfortable with

Since you only have to do one question out of three, you should have a more focused approach to your studying and pick a few topics you are comfortable and confident with. For example, if you have a strong interest in criminal law, you should focus on doing your research in that area, and if a question relevant to criminal law comes out, you will be confident and well-prepared to answer it well. Of course, you cannot predict what three topics might come out, hence it is strongly advisable for you to prepare more than just one topic, but you should not be spending too much time on topics you have no interest in or struggle to understand – for example, if you do not understand company law and have no confidence in answering an essay question on it, it might be a better use of your time in focusing on other topics for the CLT.

Marking

The CLT is marked on a scale of 1-10. The Faculty of Law Cambridge Law Test page provides a marking scheme for the CLT, with 7 being 'probably worth an offer' – hence, candidates should strive for at least a 7 to stand a good chance of receiving an offer. The criteria stated in the marking scheme includes being able to: i) identify and engage with the issues raised by the question and to critically analyse and evaluate; ii) be clear in your writing; iii) explaining your reasons in a clear and logical manner; and iv) writing in a coherent, well-structured and balanced manner.

Sample Questions

There are two sample CLT papers freely available online: **www.uniadmissions.co.uk/cambridge-law-test-mock-papers**

Maximising your One Hour

An hour passes by really quickly, and you should maximise your hour in order to write the best essay you can within the limited time frame. Whilst it is tempting to jump straight to answering a question the moment the test starts, you run the huge risk of not reading the question properly, or not having a proper plan in mind.

Remember – you are not marked solely based on your content alone. Your clarity of expression, your structure, and how concise and clear your argument is, all play a big part in differentiating between a good essay worth 7 or more on the scale and a bad one that will make you lose your offer!

Take at least five minutes at the start to properly plan your essay, especially your introduction and conclusion – sometimes a strong introduction and conclusion can make up for a weak essay! An ideal introduction will set out clearly the points you will be making and direct the examiner accordingly instead of leaving them to guess what is your argument.

One final point is that it is better to have a shorter essay that is clear and to the point than a longer essay that is confusing and all over the place – quality over quantity!

How to write your Essay

As mentioned in the assessment criteria provided by the Faculty of Law, not only is the content of your essay important, you will have to ensure that the structure is clear and easy to follow, your arguments are made in a succinct and coherent manner, and you have truly engaged with the question and shown critical analysis.

You have a total of one hour to write your essay, so make sure you utilise this time wisely and properly set out your structure beforehand to ensure that you keep on track as you are writing the essay and do not go off on a tangent or forget to address the question directly. A common mistake is that students tend to get carried away as they are writing an essay, and forget to always refer back to what the question is asking. An essay may be brilliantly written but if it does not answer the exact question, it is going to be a failing mark.

This is how you should allocate your time accordingly:

First 5 minutes	• Choose your question wisely - only pick something that you are familiar and confident with, and make sure you have fully understood what the question is asking
Next 5 minutes	• Plan out your essay by thinking about your structure • Set out your main arguments on a rough paper in point form so you do not forget them as you go along
Next 40 minutes	• Write the essay and make sure you always answer the question being asked and do not get carried away • Make sure at all times what you are writing is clear, coherent and provides a good analysis of the question
Last 10 minutes	• Give yourself ample time to check through your answer to ensure that there are no grammatical and spelling mistakes • Giving yourself ample time to finish will also ensure that you do not hand in a rushed essay with no conclusion

Structuring your Essay

The structure of an essay can be broken down into three key elements – the introduction, the main body and the conclusion.

The main body is further split into 2-4 paragraphs that provide different key points to bolster your main argument, as well as addressing the relevant counter-arguments and showing why the counter-arguments fail to undermine your main argument.

The Cambridge Law Test is unique in the sense that there are two distinct types of essay questions: a descriptive essay or a problem question.

A descriptive essay will be one that usually challenges you to think about a particular area of law, such as 'What do you think about the law of murder?'. Such essays will tend to have a rather straightforward structure of introduction-main body-conclusion that you are familiar with. In such essay questions, it will be advisable to set out your main argument in the introduction early on so as to not leave the examiner 'guessing' throughout the essay what you are trying to argue. There are usually no right and wrong answer, and in fact sometimes candidates stand out and do exceptionally well by putting forward a difficult and controversial argument, and go on to explain it really well and provide a highly convincing defence against the counter-arguments that can be raised. Avoid being overly one-sided and only raise points that are supportive of your main argument in the main body, a good essay should address and acknowledge the relevant counter-arguments that can be raised, and then go on to show how these counter-arguments are weaker than the main argument being put forward.

A problem question, on the other hand, will provide you with a pattern of facts and ask you to analyse the problem and come up with a legal solution. Such questions can be phrased differently – they can come up as a single paragraph of a narrative which will invite you to pick apart the issues separately, or they can come up in parts and you will have to address each part separately. For problem questions, there is usually no 'main argument' that you would expect for a descriptive essay, as what the examiner is looking for will be whether you are able to meticulously pick up all the different issues mentioned in the question, analyse them in a relevant manner, and come up to a final conclusion about the legal position of the parties involved based on the overall fact situation. For such questions, the steps taken and the overall analysis shown will be a lot more important that your final conclusion reached, as long as you can justify it (just as how a lawyer is expected to present the best case for his or her client no matter which side of the deal or case they are on!).

The structure of a descriptive essay can be shown as follows:

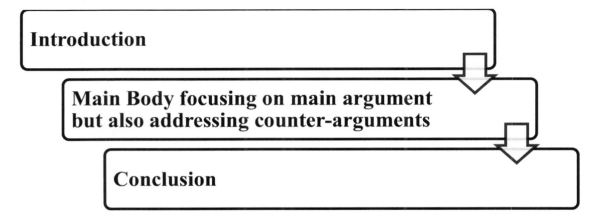

~ 102 ~

In contrast, the structure of a problem question is as follows:

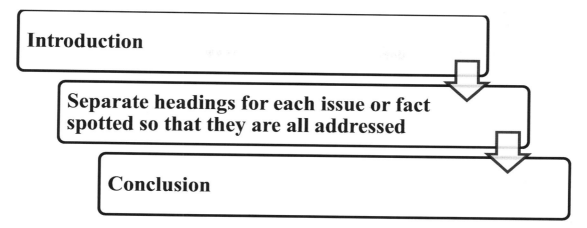

The Exam Approach

The vast **majority of problems are caused by a lack of planning and essay selection** – usually, because students just want to get writing as they are worried about finishing on time. Always resist the temptation of writing your essay straightaway without putting in thought as to how to structure your essay and to set out your arguments clearly and succinctly. A well-structured, clear and coherent essay will always be better than a longer, but more muddled essay which is hard for an examiner to follow.

Here is a summary of the correct exam approach:

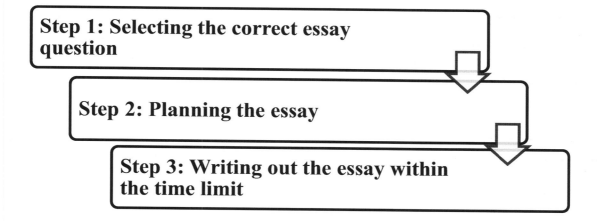

Step 1: Selecting an essay question

You will be given a choice of 3 essays to choose from and crucially, you will have no idea of what it could be beforehand. Selecting your essay is crucial- make sure you're comfortable with the topic and ensure you understand the actual question. The most fatal mistake you can make is to write an entire essay without once answering the exact question asked – **always** ensure that you fully understand a question before you attempt it. If are unsure what the question is really asking, it is usually a clear sign that you should not be attempting that question.

Take your time to read all the questions and decide which one you understand the most and will be most confident in. Whilst one essay might originally seem the easiest, if you haven't thought through it, you might quickly find yourself running out of ideas. Likewise, a seemingly difficult essay might actually offer you a good opportunity to make interesting points. If you perform well in a difficult essay as opposed to writing an average essay for an easier question, it also usually reflects well on you as examiners tend to give credit for students who attempt questions that are more challenging and successfully write a strong essay for it. Of course, you should not risk doing this if you do not understand the question fully – in that case you should stick to topics that you are comfortable with.

Use this time to carefully select which question you will answer by gauging how accessible and comfortable you are with it given your background knowledge.

It's surprisingly easy to change a question into something similar, but with a different meaning. Thus, you may end up answering a completely different essay title. Once you've decided which question you're going to do, read it very carefully a few times to make sure you fully understand it. Answer all aspects of the question. Keep reading it as you answer to ensure you stay on track!

Step 2: Planning

The importance of planning

The temptation to write an essay the minute you spot a question that you are familiar with is great, but you should always take some time initially to create a rough plan for your essay. This is not only crucial for setting out a good structure that provides a clear answer that is easy to read, this will also prevent you from getting carried away writing your essay that you forget what main points you are going to make or fail to answer the question whilst writing the essay. Remember, here are some things that the examiners look out for in a good CLT essay:

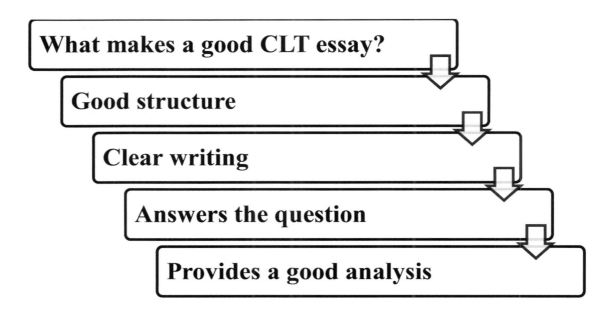

On the flip side of the coin, you should not take too much time planning your essay and leave yourself short of time when you are writing out your essay! As a rough guide, you should spend no more than 10 minutes planning an essay – the CLT is rather time-pressured as you only get an hour to write your essay, and this includes reading time, hence you need to give yourself some allowance of time in reading the questions, selecting a question and planning for it accordingly.

What does planning entail?

Planning differs from every individual, but in general make sure you think about what are the main points you will be raising in the main body and number them accordingly, ensure that you have thought about the possible counter-arguments that can be made against your essay and how you are going to tackle them, as well as how you are going to write your introduction for an effective and succinct start to your essay.

Remember – there are two different types of essay questions in the CLT, hence your planning might differ depending on which question you choose to do. For example, for a more problem question-style essay, you should focus on planning out how you are going to address every single issue you can spot in the question, and if the question is split into parts, you should perhaps think about how they are interlinked. Always keep in mind the general structure of an essay and plan accordingly:

Introduction : How am I answering the question and what points will I make?

Main body: How many points will I be making and how am I going to address my counter-arguments/have I identified all the issues mentioned in the question?

Conclusion: How can I effectively sum up what my argument is or what my final conclusion is having analysed all the issues raised?

Step 3: Writing

Introduction

The introduction should explain the statement and define any key terms. Here, you can say what you're going to say and suggest (either affirmatively or tentatively) a response or answer to the question. It is always a good idea to set out clearly what your thesis is going to be – for example whether you agree or disagree with the statement and your reasons for agreeing or disagreeing. This will tell the examiner straightaway what your opinion is instead of leaving them to guess what your point is – it does not reflect well on you when the examiners are unable to grasp what you are trying to argue!

It is important not to spend too long on an introduction as that would use up too much time unnecessarily, which could be better spent on other parts of the essay. But bear in mind the fact that a good, clear and succinct introduction sets a very good impression for an examiner and might pull up your marks.

In summary, this is what you should include in your introduction:

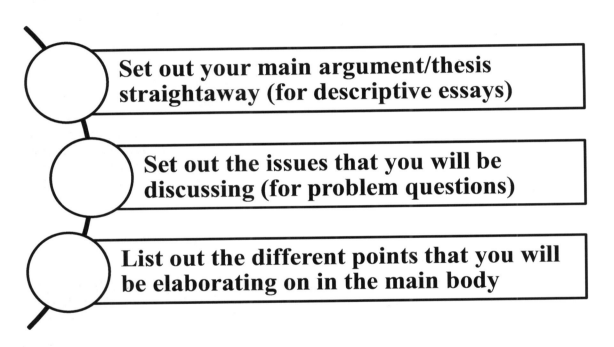

Set out your main argument/thesis straightaway (for descriptive essays)

Set out the issues that you will be discussing (for problem questions)

List out the different points that you will be elaborating on in the main body

Main Body

The importance of plain, simple English

The purpose of your essay is to show how you are able to provide a good analysis of the question asked, raise relevant examples, identify as many issues as possible, as well as to tackle any possible counterarguments. Using superfluous and flamboyant language and vocabulary will not get you far – you will have to adopt a precise, academic-style of writing for the CLT.

Tone and style

Unlike other essay-based subjects that you might have done, you should not be adopting an aggressive or overly-emotional style of writing for the CLT – you should be adopting a neutral tone and seek to provide a good analysis of the question in a legalistic manner. Avoid adopting a style that reads more like a novel or a personal blog as opposed to an academic piece of writing. If you are in doubt, you should read more newspaper articles from a credible source (e.g. Financial Times, The Economist) in order to have a feel of what a precise style of writing should be.

Structure

It is common for students to start the first paragraph of their main body by addressing the counter-argument first, so they can focus on beefing up the points in favour of their main argument in the subsequent paragraphs. Another approach adopted is to start off with your strongest points first. Whichever style you adopt, make sure you do not run out of time and fail to include the points that are most important for you to answer the question well.

Headings

Headings are optional, but they can be useful in providing a signpost for the examiner so as to understand what are the different arguments you are raising. Headings are especially useful for problem questions, as they allow you to map out all the different issues you have spotted in the question and help you ensure that you have addressed them all.

Legalistic terms

Since no prior legal knowledge is expected of students taking the CLT, you do not have to worry about trying to incorporate precise legal terms in your essay (especially Latin terms!). Whilst it is good if you are aware of the terms and how they are used precisely, avoid using them if you are unsure about their exact meaning as this might backfire on you, especially if you use a complex legal term wrongly and skew the whole meaning of your essay.

Remember these few points in order to write out a good main body, which forms the bulk of your essay:

Structure
- Make sure your paragraphs are not too long
- Headings may be useful to signal what your different arguments are

Style &Tone
- Avoid an overly casual tone
- Use precise, clear English

Content
- Always answer the question and raise relevant examples when appropriate
- Make sure you have elaborated sufficiently o each of your point to support your argument

Conclusion

Finally, this is where you can catch your breath and pat yourself on the back for a job well done! However, many students tend to neglect the conclusion, either because they run out of time or they simply do not know what to include. A good conclusion provides a good overall impression of your essay on the examiner and can go a long way in helping you achieve a good mark.

Summary of your argument

You will want to provide a good summary of your argument in order to reiterate what your main argument is and how you arrived at the conclusion. For a problem question, you will want to state your overall legal advice or solution based on the fact pattern provided.

Short and sweet

Your conclusion should only be a short, final concluding paragraph. Do not use this paragraph to introduce new ideas – any new points should be included in the main paragraph! Also avoid merely repeating what you have stated in the introduction, this is a good opportunity for you to write a short, punchy conclusion that leaves an impression on the examiner and helps to drive home the main argument you are trying to make.

FULLY WORKED ESSAYS

Example Essay 1

Who should not be allowed to serve on the jury and why?

Better Response:

Individuals who are at risk of undermining the public confidence of the criminal justice system, as well as individuals who are likely to not exercise independent judgment when serving as a juror should not be allowed to serve on the jury. The former includes individuals who have a conflict of interest with a particular case, such as a police officer who has worked on a similar case before and might have a vested interest. The latter includes individuals who have shown that they possess a certain prejudiced viewpoint, such as being more sceptical of certain religious groups.

It might be arguable that we should ban all individuals who are connected to the criminal justice system from serving as jurors. This would include several members such as judges, magistrates, police officers, solicitors and barristers. However, we run the risk of depriving many of these individuals who might be willing and able to serve as jury members. The concern that they will allow their own legal knowledge to influence their decision is valid, as the idea of a jury system is to let the jury members assess a case based on its facts, with the judge directing the jury accordingly as to what the law is. However, this is a broad generalisation and these individuals are capable of exercising independent judgment, especially if they are legally-trained as all the more they are expected to know the role of the jury and how they should go about deciding the case as a jury member. The only exception we should make are individuals who might have a vested interest in the case, such as a police officer who has worked on a similar case before, as the police officer might be tempted to decide the current case similarly. Such individuals should not be allowed to serve as a jury member on that particular case (as opposed to a general ban), in order to uphold the public's confidence in the jury system as the public expects the jury system to be independent.

There are also arguments that we should have a proportionate representation in the jury so that minority groups are well-represented. For example, we have to ensure that the jury system is not just made up fully of a certain race, religion or social background. However, whilst this is a valid sentiment, this is largely unworkable as we will have to create an artificial situation where out of 12 jury members, we will have to ensure that there is one member of each minority group. The purpose of the jury system is to ensure that the public is represented in the jury system and the jury is able to exercise independent, value-free judgement in order to decide upon a defendant's guilt based on the facts of the case. If the defendant is part of a minority group, it is a valid concern that the jury might not be sensitive to the defendant's background if they are comprised entirely of a different racial or religious group. However, the solution to this is to ensure that jurors are adequately informed and prepped beforehand, so as to ensure that they know that any judgments made in favour or against the defendant should never be based on prejudice or stereotype. If it is discovered during the initial screening process that a certain potential juror exhibits a strong tendency to have a biased opinion, then such a juror should be removed.

In conclusion, we should only disallow someone from being a juror member if there is a significant risk of conflict of interest, such as a member of a legal profession who has worked on a similar case before, or if there is a significant risk of a biased opinion, such as an individual who has exhibited a strong tendency to have prejudicial opinions.

Examiner's Comments:

Overall: This is a strong response – it answers the questions very directly, and provides an in-depth analysis of the thorny issues surrounding this topic, and shows a level of maturity and insight that goes beyond what is expected. This essay will likely score an 8 or 9 on the scale, and will stand a very good chance of getting an offer.

Introduction: The introduction directly answers the question and tells the examiner immediately what the author's thesis will be. It sets out nicely what will be expanded on in the main body, and has focused on the thorny issues raised by the question instead of wasting time talking about the less controversial issues such as age and mental capacity.

Main Body: The main body shows a very high level of analysis of the two thorny issues raised by the author in the introduction. Even though there are only two main paragraphs as compared to the previous response which had four, this is a perfect example of quality over quantity – it is better to have two main paragraphs which are analysed in great detail than to have four paragraphs which are merely glossed over without showing an in-depth analysis. The author is not afraid to lay out his/her opinion in controversial issues such as the issue of proportionate representation in the jury, and he/she tackles the counter-arguments well in order to bolster his/her own argument. There is no right or wrong answer, but as long as you have made a good attempt at addressing the counter-arguments and defending your own opinion, this will result in higher marks being awarded beyond the 'safe' range.

Conclusion: The conclusion once again nicely wraps up what has been argued thus far and provides a good summary to remind the examiner of the main argument being put forward in the essay.

Worse Response:

The jury has been traditionally made up of laypersons randomly selected in order to represent the public in deciding a case. Whether someone should be selected as juror or not is a subjective question and this will require us to examine all the circumstances of the case. We will have to look at factors such as someone's age, mental capacity, profession, family background, racial and religious background and sexuality.

Firstly, if someone is too young, they will not be a good fit for a jury because they will lack the necessary experience and the ability to evaluate a case with sufficient maturity. On the flip side, if someone is too old, this might impinge on their ability to pay close attention to their entire trial process, especially if their memory is not as good.

We also should not allow people with mental illnesses to serve in the jury as they will not have sufficient mental capacity to handle a trial process. Ideally, someone serving in the jury should have a sound mind, capable of exercising independent judgment.

Members of the public serving in certain sensitive or regulated professions should also be excluded from serving in the jury. For example, police officers and judges may have a conflict of interest by serving in the jury, and should be excluded so as to not affect the public's confidence in the jury system. Similarly, solicitors and barristers should also be excluded especially if they are likely to be affected by their pre-existing knowledge of the law instead of evaluating the case based on the facts and evidence presented before them.

We must also ensure that the jury accurately reflects the general public, hence there should be a diverse range of jurors from different family, religious and racial backgrounds, as well as sexuality. If all the jurors only represented a particular group, this might result in a strong risk of biasness and result in either an unfair outcome or the public losing confidence in the jury system. This is especially the case if the defendant happens to be from a minority group that is underrepresented.

Overall, the selection of a juror is very context-specific and we will have to look at several factors and criteria in order to decide whether someone should be part of the jury.

Examiner's Comments:

Overall: This is a valid essay, there are no major errors (e.g. not answering the question, major grammatical or spelling errors). However, it is a very 'safe' essay – i.e. it sits on the fence and does not answer the question directly, as evident from the introduction and conclusion. Hence, this will not achieve a very high mark, it will probably achieve a 5 or 6 on the scale, which means that it will not stand a very strong chance of getting an offer.

Introduction: The introduction does not explicitly answer the question, which is made up of two parts – 'who should not serve in the jury' and 'why?'. It is perfectly fine to define the jury system and explain how a juror is selected in the current system, but it is preferable for you to start your introduction by answering the question directly, so that the examiner knows straightaway what your stance is and how you are going to defend it in the subsequent paragraphs. Sitting on the fence, such as saying 'it depends on the circumstances' or 'we have to look at the facts' generally indicates a very 'safe' essay that does not answer the question directly, and will result in a 'safe' mark as well, meaning one that will not go beyond a 6.

Main Body: Overall, the points made in the main body are valid, perhaps rather superficial. For example, age and mental capacity and rather obvious factors that are not controversial, and it is better for you to start off your main body by tackling the more controversial issues that require more explanation, such as the background of a potential juror and members of certain professions in this case. This also ensures that in the event that you run out of time, you can skip the less controversial issues and focus your time on the topics that require more discussion. There is a lack of a more in-depth analysis of the controversial issues in this essay, and it is perhaps rather one-sided – you should always attempt at addressing the counter-arguments so as to strengthen your own argument and make it as fool-proof as possible.

Conclusion: Again, the conclusion suffers from the same problem as the introduction – it does not answer the question. A conclusion should be a good summary of your arguments thus far and this is a good point to remind the examiner again of your thesis – simply repeating that selecting a juror is 'context-specific' will not add any value to your essay.

Example Essay 2

Laws should always be created by Parliament and no one else. To what extent do you agree?

Better response:

While Parliament should solely be responsible for law-making due to the fundamental principle of separation of powers in terms of creating statutory law, there are other areas of law-making that the judiciary and executive should be given limited powers as well. For example, judges should have the power to exercise their discretion in areas where Parliament thinks judges are better-placed to exercise their judgment. This includes deciding the sentence of a defendant or determining the mental element of certain offences such as fraud which requires a lot of subjective judgment. The executive should be given limited powers for certain areas that will aid them in running the government, such as being given powers to legislate in administrative areas such as the administration of cities. This can be seen from the usage of statutory instruments.

The main reason why it is true that Parliament should be solely responsible for law-making in terms of creating statutory law is because Parliament, as the legislative body, is democratically-elected and represents the will of the population. Hence, under the idea of democratic legitimacy, Parliament is the only body who is able to create laws that create restrictions on the general public as they are merely reflecting the will of the democracy. If another body were to create statutory law, such as the judiciary or the executive, this will create the risk of unelected bodies creating laws that affect the freedom and rights of the general public and go against the fundamental idea of democratic legitimacy.

However, Parliament cannot envisage every single situation that will be governed by law and the flexibility and adaptiveness of our common law system makes it necessary for our judges to have certain limited law-making powers. For example, the idea of stare decisis (i.e. judgments by higher courts being binding and have precedential value) allows judges to have a certain law-making power in a way as they are able to decide cases that become binding authority. This is especially useful for certain context-specific cases that Parliament will not be able to envisage at the time of writing the statute. This power wielded by judges is limited as it is always up to Parliament to re-write the statute and override the decided case if they are unhappy with the judgment and think it goes against their intention. Hence, judges possess a powerful, albeit limited law-making power under the common law system and are able to decide on cases that require their discretion, including sentencing and deciding on the level of intention of a defendant.

The executive, being the body in charge of running the country as the government, are mainly enforcing the laws that have been enacted by Parliament and should technically not be allowed to create laws due to conflict of interest. However, in the interest of ensuring the smooth-running of the country, certain administrative tasks should be delegated to the executive so they can create rules that are binding and do not have to go through the onerous, lengthy process of parliamentary law-making. For example, certain administrative functions such as planning laws and town council regulations should be left to the executive as they are more familiar with the requirements, and can create binding rules accordingly such as using statutory instruments. Hence, they are provided with limited powers under a specific domain to create laws.

In conclusion, the main power of law-making should still be solely vested with Parliament, with the exception of limited powers being conferred on the judiciary and executive so as to allow them to perform their functions more effectively without impinging on the legislative domain of the legislative.

Examiner's Comments:

Overall: This essay handles the question well and gives a very thorough and nuanced analysis of why Parliament should be the only entity that creates law with important exceptions. The explanation provided shows a high level of further reading and the candidate has clearly read up a lot about constitutional law issues. This essay will likely achieve a 9 and stand a very high chance of getting an offer.

Introduction: The introduction answers the question directly and sets out the arguments the author will be putting forward, and is an effective introduction that allows the examiner to follow the main body with ease.

Main Body: The three paragraphs are easy to follow as the three main points have already been set out in the introduction, which shows clarity in structure and is one of the important criterion used to assess a Cambridge Law Test essay. The author also makes use of good examples based on his/her further reading, and has shown a good level of understanding of constitutional principles such as the idea of separation of powers and democratic legitimacy. The author has shown an impressive level of understanding and awareness that goes beyond what is typically expected of an applicant who has yet to read law. These factors all point towards the essay being deserving of a near-perfect mark.

Conclusion: The conclusion is short and effective, summarising the author's arguments and reinforcing the main thesis.

Worse response:

Parliament should not be the only entity that creates laws as judges are more well-suited to do so. Judges are legally-trained, understand the law better and are able to create laws that will protect more rights and lead to greater regulation of certain crimes. Hence, judges should also be allowed to make laws.

Parliament consists of Members of Parliament (MPs), and these MPs often do not have a legal background. Furthermore, they tend to pander to popular interest, hence they only enact laws that will help them achieve more votes, such as enforcing stricter laws against immigration because the general public is getting frustrated over the presence of more foreigners. Such law-making does not benefit the country, as these politicians are self-interested and only care about being elected again in the next cycle, and result in laws that are ineffective and do not focus on the long-term benefit of the country.

We need judges to create law as they are legally-trained and know how to create laws that will result in less crime and also create laws that offer better protection to fundamental human rights. For example, judges constantly hear many criminal cases, and know how to tweak the law accordingly to reduce the chances of criminals flouting the law. Judges also understand human rights better than politicians and know how to create laws that allow better protection of such rights, whereas politicians tend to have a more superficial and layperson understanding of human rights, such as not taking into account human rights when implementing draconian immigration laws just as a result of reacting to the general public's desire.

Hence, it is clear that judges are more well-placed to decide on what laws should be created, instead of politicians who are self-interested and do not have the requisite legal knowledge.

Examiner's Comments:

Overall: This essay unfortunately shows a lack of understanding of constitutional issues and comes across as too 'layperson'. There is no mention whatsoever of the executive, and the essay is too one-sided and fails to analyse the reason why we might insist on Parliament being the only entity capable of creating laws. There is no mention or any attempt of discussing concepts such as democratic legitimacy of the legislative, or what different roles the judiciary and executive play. This essay will not do well, and will probably receive a failing mark of 4.

Introduction: The introduction does answer the question directly, however it also becomes clear from the outset that the author does not have a sufficient understanding of the question and has gone completely off-track. When you are not confident that you fully understand a question or have read up enough about the issues surrounding a certain topic, it is strongly advisable for you to attempt another question.

Main Body: The author does adopt a sensible structure by talking about the two main points raised in the introduction separately. However, the analysis done shows a lack of understanding of fundamental constitutional principles, and no attempt at all in addressing counter-arguments which unfortunately weakens the essay by making it overly one-sided.

Conclusion: The conclusion is acceptable, but for the reasons mentioned above the essay is weak and shows a lack of understanding.

Example Essay 3

Susan undergoes plastic surgery with a renowned doctor, and the doctor is known to have a near 100% success rate. However, on the day of the surgery, the doctor was on his way to the surgery when he gets stuck in a traffic jam and this causes considerable delay and also affected his mood. During the surgery itself, the doctor performed all the procedures smoothly and skilfully, but because he was not in a good mood he does not provide the patient with extra aftercare that he usually does for his regular patients. Susan was recovering well from surgery at first, but subsequently started to develop a high fever and swiftly fell into a coma. It was discovered that she had an extremely rare bacterial infection, which resulted in her internal organs malfunctioning one after another. The doctor tried his best to reverse the situation, but because the infection was so unknown there was no cure and Susan died shortly afterwards. Discuss whether the doctor should be liable for any crime.

Better response:

I will be discussing whether the doctor is liable for murder or gross negligence manslaughter by discussing the actus reus, mens rea and any potential defences available based on the fact scenario.

Murder – Actus reus

In order for the actus reus element to be fulfilled, it must be shown that the actions of the doctor caused Susan's death. Causation has two limbs – factual and legal. Factual causation is established as but-for the doctor operating on Susan, Susan would not have suffered the rare bacterial infection. However, legal causation may not be established in this case as the fact that the doctor 'performed all the procedures smoothly and skilfully' shows that his operation was not the legally causative factor behind Susan's bacterial infection. The extremely rare bacterial infection might have happened purely out of bad luck, or maybe Susan had an unknown underlying condition that caused the infection. If the doctor could not have discovered this underlying condition even if he gave Susan the usual extra aftercare he would have given, the bacterial infection would be an intervening cause and break the chain of causation between the doctor's operation and Susan's infection which led to her death.

However, if the doctor could have discovered her underlying condition (if there was one) if he performed the extra aftercare, the chain of causation would not be broken. Overall, it is most likely that there is no legal causation between the doctor's operation and Susan's death, unless the specific fact pattern aforementioned was shown.

Murder – Mens rea

The doctor has not shown that he had the intent of killing Susan at all. He can only be held liable for murder if he had the requisite intent on top of the relevant actus reus. Therefore, since the doctor lacks both the necessary actus reus and mens rea, he will not be held liable for murder.

Gross negligence manslaughter – Actus reus

The actus reus element is the same as the element for murder – in this case the doctor's actions will not be a legally causative factor unless it was shown that the doctor should have found out about Susan's underlying condition (if she had one) because the doctor should have performed extra aftercare based on his credentials. The fact that he is known to have a near 100% rate success might mean that Susan only consulted the doctor because she was aware of his skills and the fact that he always performs extra aftercare, hence the doctor is held to a higher professional standard. However, this is more relevant for mens rea, and it is still the case that actus reus will not be showed unless the causative chain was not broken by the rare bacterial infection as explained above.

Gross negligence manslaughter – Mens rea

It must be shown that the doctor's actions reaches the threshold of 'gross negligence', which will be shown if the doctor acted so negligently as to show a blatant disregard for Susan's life. This is a high threshold and is not shown in the case as the doctor performed the surgery 'smoothly and skilfully', even though he failed to perform the extra aftercare which he normally does. The failure to perform the extra aftercare might result in a civil claim against him for breach of a professional duty of care, but it will not be enough to establish the requisite mental element for gross negligence manslaughter.

Hence, the doctor will not be liable for any offences, be it murder or manslaughter, as he does not fulfil the requisite actus reus and mens rea elements. He might however face a civil claim due to the fact that he failed to provide extra aftercare which he normally does.

Examiner's Comments:

Overall: This essay tackles the issues raised in this problem question scenario very effectively and concisely, and the fact that no prior legal knowledge is expected of a candidate makes this essay more impressive for the accuracy in its analysis of the fact pattern. The structure is also excellent as it lays down the different elements of criminal offences in a very clear manner and allows the examiner to follow the candidate's analysis in a thorough fashion. This essay will hence score a high mark of 9.

Introduction: The introduction is acceptable in laying down the two main offences the candidate will be analysing and their requisite elements. There are many ways of writing an introduction for a problem question, candidates just have to ensure that they do not end up writing an overly-long introduction with too much detail as that should be saved for the main body.

Main Body: The structure is excellent and makes it easy to follow the candidate's analysis. The candidate is also very precise in analysing the law. Do take note that since no prior legal knowledge is required before taking the CLT, we do not expect exact precision in knowing the law, especially when candidates are unfamiliar with the relevant statutory provisions and key cases. However, we do want to see an attempt at tackling **all** the issues raised in the fact scenario and a sensible analysis of what the law would say.

Conclusion: The conclusion is again acceptable and candidates should usually just summarise what their stand is and keep it concise and clear.

Worse response:

Doctor has near 100% successful rate – this means that the doctor is held to a higher standard and should be liable if he fails to achieve the high standard that he is held to. Doctor was stuck in a traffic jam which caused considerable delay and affected his mood – this will not be an excuse for the doctor as being in a bad mood does not result in the standard he is measured against being lowered, he will still be liable for Susan's death even if he was affected by the traffic jam.

Performed all procedures smoothly and skilfully but did not provide extra aftercare – since the doctor is known to provide patients with extra aftercare, the fact that he failed to provide aftercare to Susan increases his guilt as doing so might have prevented Susan from getting infected.

Extremely rare bacterial infection – while this may have been the cause of Susan's death instead of the actual operation itself, the fact that this could have been prevented if the doctor performed the extra aftercare means that the doctor should still be held liable.

Doctor tried his best to reverse the situation – This would have been too late following the infection, and this might be a mitigating factor in the doctor's defence but does not change the fact that the doctor's negligence in failing to provide aftercare caused Susan's death. Hence, the doctor should still be held liable.

Therefore, the doctor should be convicted for causing Susan's death.

Examiner's Comments:

Overall: This is not a bad essay per se, but it leaves a lot of room for improvement. The good thing is that the candidate made an attempt at addressing every issue mentioned in the problem by going through them one by one chronologically. However, the candidate's answer did not go into enough depth, and did not consider the different kinds of offences that might be available besides just murder. This will be a passing mark, but just barely, so it will score a 5.

Introduction: There is a lack of introduction here, which is not fatal but it would help to set out a simple introduction setting out what offences you will analyse and the elements that need to be established.

Main Body: The structure works because it ensures that every single issue in the question is addressed. However, it also makes it harder for the examiner to check whether the candidate has fully analysed the different elements of the crime because some issues mentioned may be connected and hence dealing with them separately may not be the most sensible option sometimes. The candidate also needs to go more in-depth for certain issues that require more thorough analysis, such as the rare bacterial infection being a possible intervening cause.

Conclusion: The conclusion is really short but acceptable as it summarises the candidate's main argument.

Example Essay 4

Albert was recently retrenched from his previous job and has been actively looking for a job. One of the potential employers requested a reference from Albert's ex-employer, hence Albert contacted his ex-employer in order to receive a reference. The ex-employer, being a big multinational corporation, had to go through Human Resources (HR) in order to prepare the reference according to their standard protocol. The HR officer in charge received information that an ex-employee named Albert needed a reference, hence she did a search on her system and retrieved the information, not knowing that it was the wrong 'Albert'. The wrong information contained extremely bad reviews, as this wrong 'Albert' was notorious for being late for work, producing sloppy work and being defiant to his superiors. Hence, the real 'Albert' did not manage to secure that particular job. Discuss whether the employer should be held liable for Albert's failure to get a job, and if so, what should the extent of compensation be.

Better response:

The employer's potential liability towards Albert will depend on whether i) there is a duty of care owed to Albert; ii) the duty of care is breached; iii) the breach caused Albert's loss; and iv) Albert suffered loss as a result.

i) Duty of care

The employer owes Albert a duty of care to prepare an accurate reference, even though Albert is no longer employed by the employer. This is due to their professional relationship and there is an assumption of responsibility of the employer towards Albert, an ex-employee, to ensure that Albert's past performance and aptitude has been accurately recorded. There is a relationship of mutual trust and confidence between the employer and Albert, hence a duty of care exists and we have to move on to the next limb.

ii) Breach

There is a prima facie breach of the duty of care owed to Albert as the reference was prepared negligently (i.e. the wrong reference was given). The employer may try to raise a defence by pointing out that it was the HR officer's fault in retrieving the wrong information. However, the HR officer is an officer of the company and was acting under the instructions of the employer and carried out the search in the course of his or her work.

Hence, it is not a defence for the employer to claim that one of its officers was negligent, unless they can show that the officer acted outside their scope of work or acted fraudulently and beyond the employer's control. In this case, it is not shown that the HR officer has acted outside the scope of his or her work, nor is it shown that the HR officer has acted fraudulently and beyond the control of the employer. Hence, a breach of the duty of care is established and we can move on to the next limb.

iii) Causation

Causation consists of two elements – factual causation and legal causation. Factual causation is established in this case if it is shown that but-for the bad reference, Albert would have gotten the job. In this case, the information does not state explicitly whether Albert did not get the job because of the bad reference. For example, if Albert performed so badly in the job interview that the potential employer would not have employed Albert even if his reference was perfect, the bad reference would not be a legally causative factor and causation will not be established. Hence, it must be shown that the bad reference was a but-for cause that resulted in Albert not securing the job. Furthermore, legal causation must be established – in this case, it must be shown that the damage suffered was not too remote. The fact that Albert could not secure a job due to a bad reference is not too remote as it is within the ex-employer's expectation and understanding that an ex-employee would require a reference as a crucial part of applying for a new job, especially when the ex-employer happens to be a sophisticated multi-national corporation. Therefore, provided it is shown that the bad reference was a but-for cause, causation is established.

iv)   Loss

Finally, we have to assess the extent of Albert's loss in order to determine how much compensation the employer is liable for. A loss of a job means a loss of future earnings, and how much compensation is payable will depend on how long Albert takes to find a new job. For example, if Albert is able to swiftly secure another job after this failed attempt, this amount of compensation payable will be limited to the very short period that Albert was left unemployed after the failed job application. If, however, despite Albert's reasonable attempts, he still is unable to find a job as a result of the stigma behind his previous failed attempt, the employer will be liable to compensate Albert in the meantime for his loss of earnings.

In conclusion, provided the factors mentioned above are established, the employer is liable in tort to compensate Albert for his loss of earnings as a result of his failed job application, up until the point when he manages to secure another job.

Examiner's Comments:

Overall: This is a very solid attempt at tackling this problem question, setting out the different elements of a tort claim in a very clear and structured manner. The analysis is also very precise, with good explanations as to the legal nuances behind the different elements of the claim. This essay will easily score a 9.

Introduction: The introduction very clearly sets out what will be discussed in detail in the main body and gives the examiner a very clear roadmap as to how the essay will be structured. Hence the introduction is simple, concise and effective.

Main Body: The headings make it really easy for the examiner to follow the candidate's analysis of the possible claim and ensures that no element is left out. The candidate has also done a good job in tackling all the issues raised in the fact pattern. Remember – if a particular fact is included in the question, it is *always* there for a reason, do not leave out any parts of the question when answering such problem questions! A good exam technique will be to underline or highlight all the different facts you can spot in the question and number them, so you can check whether you have dealt with every single fact pattern accordingly.

Conclusion: The conclusion is once again short, concise and effective and summarises the candidate's thesis clearly.

Worse response:

The employer should not made to compensate Albert for not securing his job, as it is the HR officer's fault for being careless in retrieving Albert's employment information. Therefore, a claim should be brought against the HR officer instead.

The reason why the employer is not at fault is because they have done all they could to support Albert's application for a new job even though Albert was no longer part of the company. The company took the time, money and effort to instruct their relevant HR department to prepare a reference for Albert. This was all they had to do and any mistakes made afterwards are solely the HR officer's fault and Albert's fault as well.

The HR officer of a big multi-national corporation should have the necessary skills and experience to handle producing references for ex-employees. Therefore a high standard is expected of a HR officer and a serious mistake such as retrieving the wrong information just because the ex-employee happened to have the same name as someone else is no excuse for the HR officer.

It is also partly Albert's fault for not checking with the HR officer to ensure that the right reference was sent, as he is the one that wanted to apply for the job after all and hence was the one that stood to lose out the most. Therefore, the HR officer should not be fully liable for Albert's loss, and Albert should be responsible to the extent that he failed to ensure the right reference was sent.

Hence, the HR officer will be partly liable for Albert's loss, with Albert being personally responsible for the part of the loss that is attributable to his carelessness.

Examiner's Comments:

Overall: Unfortunately, this essay has not analysed the question well enough and does not show a satisfactory level of understanding of the potential issues behind this question. Even if no prior knowledge is needed, the candidate has failed to show general awareness of the corporate world and failed to appreciate the fact that a company generally cannot absolve themselves of liability just because one of their department made a mistake, if the department is part of the company. The candidate has also made another fundamental mistake of assuming that Albert had the ability to check the reference to begin with – most references are sent confidentially and the applicant will not have a chance to look at it at all, similarly to a Cambridge application! This will be a failing mark of 3 due to the fundamental misunderstandings.

Introduction: The introduction is acceptable, ignoring the misunderstandings the candidate has made. However, for such problem questions, you do not necessarily have to come up with your final answer straightaway in the introduction as opposed to general essays – the examiner is more interested in seeing the steps in your analysis and sometimes there is no right or wrong final answer anyway.

Main Body: The structure is slightly muddled and because of that the candidate fails to address certain key facts mentioned in the question, as well as tackle the different elements behind a tort claim effectively. This is an example where a clear structure might have saved the essay and made it a passing mark, despite the fundamental misunderstandings that have been made.

Conclusion: The conclusion is acceptable as it sets out the candidate's final answer clearly, despite the misunderstandings made.

Example Essay 5

Should the courts allow a child to refuse a blood transfusion because he is a Jehovah's Witness, even though without the blood transfusion the child will die?

Better response:

The court should only allow a child to refuse consent to blood transfusion if the consent is genuine, informed and made with a sound mind. Most of the time, a child would not fulfil this criteria as the child will lack the maturity and capability of forming consent regarding such an important matter, and hence the courts will have to override the child's desire and order the life-saving blood transfusion to be carried out. However, in the exceptional situation where a child shows sufficient maturity to be able to make an informed decision, the court should not override the child's desire.

Firstly, whether a consent can be genuine and informed must be assessed based on whether the child has made the decision after considering the gravity of the situation, and has arrived at an independent, mature judgment that is not heavily influenced by his or her parents' desire. This is a very high threshold to be reached, and most children will lack the necessary maturity level to be able to reach an independent, informed decision regarding a matter of life and death. Hence, in the interest of the child and to ensure that the child continues to live, it is always in the best interest for the court to override the child's apparent wishes and to order the life-saving treatment to be carried out. The actual age of the child does not matter as much as the level of maturity displayed by the child, as different children mature differently and a 14-year-old might show the maturity level of an adult and vice versa.

Secondly, if in the exceptional situation where a child has shown sufficient maturity and capability to make an informed decision of upholding one's religious belief and refusing to accept a blood transfusion, the court should not order the blood transfusion to be carried out. This is because an invasive surgery such as a blood transfusion should never be carried out against a patient's wishes as this would be intruding on the patient's autonomy to his or her own body and doing so might constitute a crime as the patient would be deliberately harmed in the process against their consent.

This is similarly to patients being able to opt out of potentially life-saving operations if they refuse to be treated for various reasons – for example they might not want to drag out their suffering if they are suffering from a terminal illness, or they do not want to run the risk of the operation failing. It is under the doctors' Hippocratic Oath to act in the patient's best interests, but the patient's consent ultimately still trumps any potential operation that can be done on the patient, subject to such consent being informed and independently-made. Hence, a stringent test will have to be carried out to ensure that the child has made an informed and independent decision, and as explained above this will be a very high threshold to establish to prevent abuse.

Hence, in conclusion, it is nearly always the case that the court should order the life-saving blood transfusion to be carried out on the child, subject to the exceptional circumstance where it can be established that the threshold has been established and the child has made an independent and informed decision not to accept the blood transfusion.

Examiner's Comments:

Overall: This response provides a nuanced and analytical approach to the question, and also made a very sensible suggestion as to why there might be exceptional circumstances where we might have to accept that the child refuses to receive the blood transfusion. Due to the added level of analysis and nuance, this essay will score well and will most likely score an 8 or 9.

Introduction: The introduction directly answers the question and clearly sets out the two main arguments that will be raised in the main body, hence showing the candidate has thought about how to structure his or her essay before writing it out.

Main Body: The two main paragraphs deal with two distinct points that have been elaborated in great detail and has shown a very deep level of analysis. Again, this is another example of quality over quantity, even though this response has only raised two main arguments as opposed to the previous response, the level of deeper analysis is preferred over a more shallow treatment of many different points.

Conclusion: The conclusion nicely summarises the candidate's argument and reminds the examiner why there might be exceptional circumstances where the court should allow the child to refuse the blood transfusion.

Worse response:

The court should never allow someone to refuse a blood transfusion because a person's life is more important than one's religious beliefs. Therefore, if the blood transfusion was life-saving, the child will not be able to refuse it on the grounds of religion.

Life is sacrosanct and without the right to live, the child would not be able to enjoy other rights, such as right to religious freedom. Hence, in such a scenario where the right to pursue one's religious beliefs directly conflicts with one's right to live, the right to live takes precedence and the child should not be allowed to refuse the blood transfusion.

There is also the issue of the child being too young to be able to decide what religion he or she wishes to adhere to. This risks the child not having a say regarding whether or not to receive a life-saving treatment, as the child may just be repeating what his or her parents have told him or her regarding their religious belief without forming an independent thought as to whether the belief is so important that they should refuse a life-saving treatment.

Even though the parents have parental control over the child, parents do not have absolute control over their children's lives – e.g. parents are not allowed to harm their children. Hence, if the parents convinced the child that their religious belief disallows any form of blood transfusion even though it is a life-saving treatment, this is tantamount to harming the child as this puts the child at risk of dying. In the interest of the child's life, the court should override the parents' wishes and allow the hospital to let the child undergo a blood transfusion to save the child's life.

Even though we live in a society that tolerates religious freedom and expression, we should draw a line when doing so results in harm and danger to a child. This is a case where the right to freedom of expression of religion causes an actual risk to a child's life, and hence we cannot tolerate such an expression of religious freedom because the child's life has absolute priority.

Therefore, in conclusion, the court should not allow the child to refuse consent to the blood transfusion and the child's life takes priority over the child's religion.

Examiner's Comments:

Overall: This is a reasonable attempt at tackling the question, and this essay definitely answers the question directly. It comes across as being slightly one-sided at times, and the candidate could have achieved higher marks by addressing the counter-arguments more in order to bolster his or her own argument. The structure is clear enough for the examiner to follow the candidate's argument. Overall, this essay will achieve an above average mark of 6 to 7.

Introduction: The introduction directly answers the question and hence provides a good starting point. However, the candidate should also have taken this opportunity to set out the main arguments that will be expanded on in the main body so that the examiner knows from the outset what will be the three main points raised by the candidate.

Main Body: The main body is well-structured and sets out three distinct points clearly with sufficient analysis and explanation. As mentioned above, more could be done with regards to raising counter-arguments and addressing them effectively, so as to not make the essay overly one-sided. Headings could also be used in this case to set out clearly what the three main points are, since this has not already been done in the introduction.

Conclusion: The conclusion is effective and summarises the candidate's main argument.

For 10 more example essays check *The Ultimate CLT Guide*– flick to the back to get a free copy.

OXBRIDGE INTERVIEWS

The Basics

What is an Oxbridge Interview?

An interview is a personal 20-30 minute session with one or two members of academic staff from Oxford or Cambridge. The interviewers will ask questions and **guide the applicant to an answer**. The answers usually require a large degree of creative and critical thought, as well as a good attitude and a sound foundation of subject-specific knowledge.

Why is there an Interview?

Most of the applicants to Oxbridge will have outstanding grades, predicted exam results, sample course work and personal statements. Interviews are used to help **determine which applicants are best-suited** for Oxbridge. During the interview, each applicant has a unique chance to demonstrate their creativity and critical thinking abilities- skills that Oxford and Cambridge consider vital for successful students.

Who gets an Interview?

At Cambridge, any applicant who might have a chance at being accepted to study will be called for interview. This corresponds to approximately **90%** of applicants. At Oxford, a slightly smaller **40-80%** of applicants are interviewed (applicants are shortlisted based on their admissions test results and UCAS form). No one is offered a place to study without attending an interview.

Who are the interviewers?

The interviews are conducted by a senior member of staff for the subject you've applied to; usually this person is the **Director of Studies** for that subject. There may also be a second interviewer who takes notes on the applicant or also asks questions. Interviewers describe this experience as just as nerve-wracking for them as for the applicants, as they are responsible for choosing the right students for Oxford and Cambridge.

When is the Interview?

Interviews are held in the **beginning of December** and some applicants may be invited back in January for a second round of interviews at another college. There are usually multiple interviews on the same day, either for different subjects or at different colleges. You will normally be given 2 weeks' notice before your interview- so you should hear back by late November, but it is useful to **begin preparing for the interview before you're officially invited**.

Where is the Interview?

The interviews are held in Oxford and Cambridge **at the college you applied to**. Oxford applicants may have additional interviews at another college than the one applied to. Cambridge applicants may get 'pooled' – be required to have another set of interviews in January at a different college. If you are travelling from far away, most Oxbridge colleges will provide you free accommodation and food for the duration of your stay if you wish to arrive the night before your interview.

Very rarely, interviews can be held via Skype at an exam centre- this normally only applies to international students or for UK students in extreme circumstances.

Oxbridge Tutorials & Supervisions

Hopefully, by this point, you're familiar with the unique Oxbridge teaching system. Students on the same course will have lectures and practicals together. These are supplemented by college-based tutorials/supervisions. A tutorial/supervision is an **individual or small group session** with an academic to **discuss ideas, ask questions, and receive feedback** on your assignments. During the tutorial/supervision, you will be pushed to think critically about the material from the course in novel and innovative ways. To get the most out of Oxbridge, you need to be able to work in this setting and take criticism with a positive and constructive attitude.

The **interviews are made to be model tutorials/supervisions**, with an academic questioning an applicant and seeing if they can learn, problem-solve, demonstrate motivation for their subject. It is by considering this ultimate goal of the interview that you can start to understand how to present and prepare yourself for the Oxbridge interview process.

What Are Interviewers Looking for?

There are several qualities an interviewer is looking for the applicant to demonstrate during the interview. While an applicant may think the most 'obvious' thing interviewers are looking for is excellent factual knowledge, this is already displayed through exam results. Whilst having an excellent depth of knowledge may help you perform better during an interview, **you're unlikely to be chosen based solely on your knowledge**. The main thing an interviewer is looking for is for the applicant to demonstrate critical thought, excellent problem-solving skills and intellectual flexibility, as well as **motivation for the subject and suitability for small group teaching**. It is also important for them to see that the applicant is willing to persevere with a challenging problem even if the answer is not immediately apparent.

How to Communicate Answers

The most important thing to do when communicating your answers is to **think out loud**. This will allow the interviewer to understand your thought processes. They will then be able to help you out if you get stuck. You should never give up on a question; show that you won't be perturbed at the first sign of hardship as a student, and remain positive and **demonstrate your engagement with the material**. Interviewers enjoy teaching and working with students who are as enthusiastic about their subject as they are.

Try to **keep the flow of conversation going** between you and your interviewer so that you can engage with each other throughout the entire interview. The best way to do this is to just keep talking about what you are thinking. It is okay to take a moment when confronted with a difficult question or plan your approach, but ensure you let the interviewer know this by saying, *"I'm going to think about this for a moment"*. Don't take too long- if you are finding the problems difficult, the **interviewers will guide and prompt you** to keep you moving forward. They can only do this if they know you're stuck!

The **questions that you'll be asked are designed to be difficult**, so don't panic up when you don't immediately know the answer. Tell the interviewer what you do know, offer some ideas, talk about ways you've worked through a similar problem that might apply here. If you've never heard anything like the question asked before, say that to the interviewer, *"I've never seen anything like this before"* or *"We haven't covered this yet at school"*, but don't use that as an excuse to quit. This is **your chance to show that you are eager to engage with new ideas**, so finish with *"But let's see if I can figure it out!"* or *"But I'm keen to try something new!"*. There are many times at Oxbridge when students are in this situation during tutorials/supervisors and you need to show that you can persevere in the face of difficulty (and stay positive and pleasant to work with while doing so).

Types of Interviews

There are, at Cambridge and for some Oxford subjects, several different types of interview that you can be called for. **Every applicant will have at least one subject interview**. Applicants to some courses may also have a **general interview**, especially if they are applying for an arts subject. Either way, you will be asked questions that touch on the course you are applying to study. It may be useful to **look at your interviewers' teaching backgrounds and published work** as this could potentially shed some light on the topics they might choose to discuss in an interview. However, there is absolutely no need to know the intricacies of their research work so don't get bogged down in it. Interviews tend to open with easier and more general questions and become more detailed and complicated as you are pushed to explore topics in greater depth.

Using the Practice Questions

This book contains real law interview questions; **they are all actual questions that successful Oxbridge applicants were asked in their interview**. However, it is important you take these with a pinch of salt.

They are taken out of context and only included to give you a flavour of the style and difficulty of real Oxbridge interview questions. Don't fall into the trap of thinking that your interview will consist of a series of irrelevant and highly specific knowledge based questions.

Thus, it does little benefit to rote learn answers to all the practice questions in this book as they are unlikely to be repeated. Instead, follow our top tips, take inspiration from the worked answers and put in some hard work – you'll be sure to perform well on the day.

OXBRIDGE INTERVIEWS ARE <u>NOT</u> ABOUT YOUR KNOWLEDGE

**THEY ARE ABOUT WHAT YOU CAN DO
WITH THE KNOWLEDGE YOU ALREADY POSSES**

GENERAL INTERVIEWS

A general interview is a get-to-know-you session with senior admissions tutors. This is your chance to demonstrate a passion for Oxbridge; that you have understood the Oxbridge system, have a genuine interest in being a student, and could contribute to Oxbridge if you were admitted. These are more common for arts and humanities applicants, but all applicants should nevertheless be prepared for a general interview.

➤ This will be less specific than the subject interview. The interviewers will focus more on your personal statement, any essays you may have submitted or have completed on the day of the interview and may discuss your SAQ form if you are applying to Cambridge.

➤ One of the interviewers may not be a specialist in the subject you've applied for. Don't be put off by this – you aren't expected to have any knowledge of their subject.

➤ Ensure that you have read your personal statement and any books/journals that you've claimed to have read in your application. You will seem unenthusiastic and dishonest if you can't answer questions regarding topics and activities that you claim to know about. Remember that it is much better to show a good understanding of a few texts than to list lots of texts that you haven't properly read.

➤ Read and re-read the essays you have submitted. Be prepared to expand on the ideas you have explored in them. Remember, that the interviewers may criticise what you've argued in your submitted essays. If you believe in it, then defend your view but don't be stubborn.

➤ You will normally be asked if you have any questions at the end of the interview. Avoid saying things like, "*How did I do?*" – Instead use this as an opportunity to show the interviewers the type of person you are e.g. "*How many books can I borrow from the library at one time?*"

What type of questions might be asked?

The three main questions that are likely to come up in an Oxbridge interview are:

➤ *Why Oxford/Cambridge?*
➤ *Why this subject?*
➤ *Why this college?*

You may also get asked more specific questions about the teaching system or about your future career aspirations. This will also be the time for discussing any extenuating circumstances for poor exam results and similar considerations.

To do well in a general interview, your answers should show that you understand the Oxbridge system and that you have strong reasons for applying there. Thus, it is essential that you prepare detailed answers to the common questions above so that you aren't caught off guard. In addition, you should create a list of questions that could potentially be asked based on your personal statement or any submitted work.

Worked Questions

Below are a few examples of how to start breaking down general interview questions- complete with model answers.

Q1: How did you choose which college to apply for?

This question is a good opportunity to tell the interviewer about yourself, your hobbies, motivations, and any interesting projects you have undertaken. You can demonstrate that you have read about the College thoroughly and you know what differentiates your College from the others. The decisive factors can include a great variety of different things from history, alumni, location in the city, community, sports clubs, societies, any positive personal experiences from Open Day and notable scholars.

This is a warm up question – an ice-breaker – so just be natural and give an honest answer. You may not want to say things like, *"I like the statutes in the garden"*. The more comprehensive your answer is, the better.

Good Applicant: I chose which college to apply for based on a number of factors that were important to me. First of all, I needed to consider how many other students at my college would be studying the same subject as me; this was important to me as I want to be able to engage in conversation about my subject with my peers. Secondly, I considered the location of the college as I wanted to ensure I had easy access to the faculty library and lecture theatres. Thirdly, I am a keen tennis player and so looked for a college with a very active tennis society. Finally, I wanted to ensure that the college I chose would feel right for me and so I looked around several Cambridge colleges before coming to my conclusion.

This response is broken down into a set of logical and yet personal reasons. **There is no right answer to this question** and the factors which influence this decision are likely to be unique for each individual. However, each college is unique and therefore the interviewer wants to know what influenced your decision. Therefore, **it's essential that you know what makes your college special** and separates it from the others. Even more importantly, you should know what the significance of that will be for you. For example, if a college has a large number of mathematicians, you may want to say that by attending that college, it would allow you to discuss your subject with a greater number of people than otherwise.

A **poor applicant** may respond with a noncommittal shrug or an answer such as, *"my brother went there"*. The interviewers want to see that you have researched the university and although the reason for choosing a college won't determine whether or not you get into the university, a lack of passion and interest in the college will greatly influence how you are perceived by the interviewers.

Q2: Why have you chosen to apply to study at 'Oxbridge', rather than another Russell Group university?

This is a very broad question and one which is simply designed to draw out the motives and thinking behind your application, as well as giving you an opportunity to speak freely about yourself.

A **good applicant** would seek to address this question in two parts, the first addressing the key features of Oxbridge for their course and the second emphasising their own personality traits and interests which make them most suited to the Oxbridge system.

It is useful to start off by talking about the supervision/tutorial system and why this method of very small group teaching is beneficial for studying your subject, both for the discussion of essay work and, more crucially, for developing a comprehensive understanding of your subject. You might also like to draw upon the key features of the course at Oxford and Cambridge that distinguish it from courses at other universities.

When talking about yourself, a good answer could take almost any route, though it is always productive to talk about which parts of your subject interest you, why this is the case, and how this ties in with the course at Oxford/Cambridge. You might also mention how the Oxbridge ethos suits your personality, e.g. how hard work and high achievement are important to you and you want to study your chosen subject in real depth, rather than a more superficial course elsewhere.

A **poor applicant** would likely demonstrate little or no knowledge of their course at Oxford/Cambridge and volunteer little information about why studying at Oxbridge would be good for them or why they would be suited to it. It's important to focus on your interests and abilities rather than implying that you applied because Oxbridge is the biggest name or because your family or school had expected you to do so.

Q3: What will you contribute to college life?

This is a common question at general interviews and **you need to show that you would be a good fit for the College** and that you are also really motivated because you have researched the college's facilities, notable fellows and alumni, societies and sports clubs etc. You can mention that you have looked at the website, talked to alumni and current students.

This question also gives the interviewer an excellent opportunity to learn about your personality, hobbies and motivations. Try to avoid listing one thing after the other for 5 minutes. Instead, you should try to give a balanced answer in terms of talking about the College and yourself. You should talk about your skills and give examples when you had to work in a team, deliver on strict deadlines, show strong time-management skills etc. You should also give a few examples from your previous studies, competitions or extracurricular activities (including sports and music).

Q4: Tell me about a recent news article not related to your subject that has interested you.

This can be absolutely anything and your interviewers just want to see that **you are aware of the world in which you live** and have a life outside of your subject. You could pick an interesting topic ahead of time and cultivate an opinion which could spark a lively discussion.

Q5: Which three famous people would you most like to be stuck on a desert island with?

This is a personal question that might be used by your interviewers as an 'ice-breaker' – you can say absolutely anyone but try to have a good justification (and avoid being melodramatic). This is a really **good chance to show your personality and sense of humour**. This is also a good question to ease you into the flow of the interview and make yourself feel more comfortable.

Q6: Do you think you're 'clever'?

Don't let this one faze you! Your interviewers are not being glib but instead want to see how you cope with questions you may not have anticipated. You could discuss different forms of intelligence, e.g. emotional vs. intellectual, perhaps concluding that you are stronger in one over the other.

Q7: What have you done in the past that makes you think you're equipped to deal with the stresses of Oxbridge?

The **interviewers want to hear that you know what you're signing up to** and that you are capable of dealing with stress. If you have any experience of dealing with pressure or meeting strict deadlines, this would be a good opportunity to talk about them. Otherwise, mention your time management skills and your ability to prioritise workloads. You could also mention how you deal with stress, e.g. do you like running? Yoga? Piano? Etc.

Q8: Why are you sitting in this chair?

There are hundreds of potential responses to this type of question, and the interviewer will see this as a chance to get to know your personality and how you react to unusual situations.

Firstly, **take the question seriously**, even if it strikes you as funny or bizarre. A good response may begin with: "There are many reasons why I am sitting in this chair. There are lots of smaller events and causes that have led up to me sitting in this chair". You might choose to discuss your desire to attend Oxbridge, the fact that you have travelled to the college to take your interview. You might choose to discuss the interviewer or college's taste and budget when it came to selecting the chair you are sitting in, as that determined why and how you have come to be sitting in that particular chair, rather than any other chair. You might then simply mention that you were invited by the interviewer to take a seat.

A weak response to this type of question would be to dismiss it as silly or irrelevant.

Q9: If you could have dinner with anyone in the world, who would it be?

This is a fairly straightforward question to get in a general interview, so use it to show your personality and originality, and to talk about something you are really passionate about.

If you are asked a question like this, give an answer that is relevant to your application. This is not the time to start talking about how you are a huge fan of Beyonce and would just love to have dinner together! You should also avoid generic answers like "God".

If you would love to meet Obama and know more about him, consider what that would be like. Would he be at liberty to answer your questions? Might you not get more information from one of his aides or from a close friend, rather than the man himself? As this is a simple question, try to unpick it and answer it in a sophisticated way, rather than just stating the obvious.

Q10: What was the most recent film you watched?

This question seems simple and appears to require a relatively short answer. However, a good candidate will use a simple question such as this as an opportunity to speak in more depth and **raise new and interesting topics of conversation**: "What I find particularly interesting about this film was…. It reminded me of….. In relation to other works of this period/historical context, I found this particular scene very interesting as it mirrored/contrasted with my previous conceptions of this era as seen in other works, for example… I am now curious to find out more about… This film made me think about…etc."

Whilst it is extremely important to respond accurately to the questions posed by the interviewer, do not be afraid to **take the conversation in the direction led by your personal interests**. This sort of initiative will be encouraged.

Q11: How should we measure your success at the end of your time here?

This question invites you to show your potential and how diverse your interests are. There are three aspects of this question that you should consider in order to give a complete answer: "end of your time here", "measure" and "your achievements". You may want to discuss your hobbies and interests and potential achievements regarding various aspects of university life including academia, sports, student societies, jobs, volunteering etc.

Then you may want to enter into a discussion about whether there is any appropriate measure of success. How could you possibly compare sporting excellence to volunteering? Is it better to be a specialist or a generalist? This ultimately comes down to your personal motivation and interests as you might be very focused on your studies or other activities (e.g. sports, music). Thus, multiple things would contribute to your success at university and your degree is only likely to be one way to measure this. Finally, it might be a great closing line to mention that getting your degree might not be the "end of your time here".

Q12: Why should anyone go to university?

This sounds like a very general question at first but it is, in fact, about your personal motivations to go to university. You don't need to enter into a discussion about what universities are designed for or any educational policy issues as the interviewer is unlikely to drive the discussion towards this in a general interview.

The best strategy is to **discuss your motivations**- this could include a broad range of different things from interest in a certain field, inspiring and diverse environments, academic excellence, opening up of more opportunities in the future and buying time to find out more about yourself etc. As it is very easy to give an unfocused answer, you should limit yourself to a few factors. You can also comment on whether people should go to university and whether this is good for the society.

Q13: How would you describe this painting on the wall to your friend on the phone?

This question is very common and surprisingly difficult. **You can take a number of approaches**. Ensure that you have a concrete idea of the structure you will use to describe the painting. For example, you could begin with your personal feelings about it, then the colours and atmosphere the painting creates, then the exact objects, then their respective position and size. It does not matter which approach you take but this question is designed to test your way of organising and presenting your ideas.

You could also comment on the difficulty of the task and argue that human language limits you from adequately describing smell, taste, sound, and vision. Modern language applicants may have read about Wittgenstein, in which case, they can reference his works on the limitations and functions of language here.

Q14: Which person in the past would you most like to interview, and why?

This is a personal question but try to **avoid generic and mainstream answers**. Keep in mind that you can find out much more about a particular period or era by speaking to everyday citizens or advisors for politicians or other important figures. It is much more important to identify what you want to learn about and then set criteria to narrow down the possible list of persons. This question opens the floor for developing an analytical, quasi-scientific approach to your research.

Q15: Tell me about a recent news article that interested you.

Whilst this question may be asked at a general interview, it's a good idea to come up with something that is related to your course. Instead of going into technical detail with an interviewer who may be from a completely different discipline, it is better to give a brief overview of the article and then put it into a broader context.

For example, an economics applicant may want to discuss the decision of the Swiss National Bank to discontinue the currency 'ceiling'.

Definition: The currency ceiling was a policy to peg the value of the Franc to the Euro at a rate of 1.2.

Reasons: At the beginning of the Euro crisis, investors turned away from the more risky Euro and started buying Francs instead which was then perceived as a stable currency. This resulted in the value of the Franc increasing with respect to other currencies, especially the Euro. But this had a negative impact on the Swiss economy as a strong currency is not favourable for export.

Analyse the news: The decision of the National Bank to let the exchange change freely will certainly cause harm to the Swiss economy. On the other hand, it will cost the National Bank a lot of money to maintain the 1.2 Franc:Euro exchange rate by buying Euros and selling Francs in the open market. And the Swiss National Bank had a large exposure to Euro, with its risks.

The answer should not be a complete analysis of the issue but an intuitive and logical description of an event. Then the interviews would most likely ask you to make recommendations or ask your opinion about the whole article.

General Interview Questions:

The following pages contain real examples of interview questions that our tutors were asked at their **general interview**. At first glance, they may appear rather obscure and intimidating. However, remember that you are unlikely to be asked these questions in series. They will only be asked because the topic being discussed naturally led to the question or if you alluded to it earlier. E.g. *"Why are flowers not green?"* may precede or follow a discussion of chlorophyll or the evolution of colour vision.

Thus, whilst going through these questions is excellent practice, ensure that you don't get too bogged down in the knowledge aspects of these questions.

Interviewers are far more interested to see what you can do with the knowledge you already possess.

1. What do you expect to get out of this degree?
2. Why do you want to study [insert subject here]?
3. Why do you want to come to this college?
4. Have you been to this college before?
5. What makes you think this University will be the right fit for you?
6. Where do you see yourself in 10 years' time? What about 20 years?
7. What extracurricular activities do you do?
8. How will you contribute to College life?
9. What do you know about the course structure?
10. What is your biggest weakness?
11. What is your biggest strength?
12. How will your experiences from the Duke of Edinburgh scheme benefit your future studies?
13. What makes you want to come here when you would most certainly get a better result at any other university?
14. Oxford is very intense, how will you manage your time to deal with all of the work?
15. What did you read this morning?
16. What is the biggest challenge you've faced and how did you deal with it?
17. Who was your best teacher? How have they influenced you?
18. What are your long term plans in life?
19. What are your top three skills?
20. Would you choose a party over an essay?
21. Who's the most influential: Obama, Merkel or Adele?
22. What colour best represents you?
23. What shape is man? What shape is time?
24. Why do things have names?
25. What international newspapers and publications do you read?
26. Can you hear silence?
27. How many golf balls can you fit in a Boeing 747 plane?
28. How many planes are flying over London right now?
29. How many letters does Royal Mail deliver every day?
30. How much should you charge to wash all the windows in London?
31. How many piano tuners are there in Europe?
32. India introduces a new population control policy to address the gender imbalance. If a couple has a girl, they may have another child. If they have a boy, they can't have any more children. What would be the new ratio of boys : girls?
33. Why are manhole covers round?
34. How many times per day does a clock's hand overlap?
35. You are shrunk down so you're the size of a matchstick and then put into a blender with metal blades. It is about to be turned on – what do you do?
36. You are given 7 identical balls and another ball that looks the same as the others but is heavier than them. You can use a balance only two times. How would you identify which is the heavy ball?
37. What is your favourite number?

SUBJECT INTERVIEWS

Subject interviews are where subject-specific questions are asked to test critical thinking and problem-solving skills. These interviews are very likely to follow the format of tutorials/supervisions. You will be interviewed by one or two senior academics from the college you applied to. They will be experts on the subject you've applied for and will ask academic questions around a central theme. **The questions are intended to be difficult** so as to push you and test your critical thinking abilities in a learning situation. You are not meant to know the answers, but to use your existing knowledge to offer creative and original thoughts to address the questions.

Here are some general tips to keep in mind:

➢ Apply the knowledge you have acquired at A-Level and from your wider reading to unfamiliar scenarios.

➢ **Stand your ground if you are confident in your argument**- even if your interviewers disagree with you. They may deliberately play the devil's advocate to see if you are able to defend your argument.

➢ However, if you are making an argument that is clearly wrong and are being told so by the interviewers - then concede your mistake and revise your viewpoint. Do not stubbornly carry on.

➢ Remember, making mistakes is no bad thing. The important point is that you address the mistake head on and adapt the statement, with their assistance where necessary.

➢ The **tutors know what subjects you have studied at A-Level** so don't feel pressured to read EVERY aspect of your subject.

You may be asked legal questions or questions from a related subject, including history, politics, or current affairs with a legal slant. None of the questions asked of you will assume any previous legal knowledge, as the interviewers understand that applicants will likely not have studied law before. Be prepared to explain why you want to study law and show through extra-curricular reading or activities how you've fostered this interest.

The interview will usually consist of a large question with many smaller sub-questions that the interviewer will ask in order to guide the applicant to an answer. The main question may seem difficult, impossible, or random at first, but take a breath and start discussing with your interviewer different ideas you have for breaking down the question into manageable pieces.

The questions are designed to be difficult to give you the chance to show your full intellectual potential.

For law, the questions will usually take one of a few possible forms based on highlighting the skills necessary to 'think like a lawyer'. Five main question types are:

➢ Observation-based questions ("tell me about...")
➢ Practical questions ("how would you decide if...")
➢ Statistical questions ("given this data...")
➢ Ethical questions ("are humans obligated to...")
➢ Questions about proximate causes (mechanism; "how does…") and ultimate causes (function; "why does…"), usually both at once.

Questions also have recurring themes which appear in many questions because they are central to jurisprudential thinking: the workings of the English legal system, problems of access to justice, the centrality of morality in legal development, the future of the legal profession, the impact of international treaties and legal institutions, looking carefully at words and drawing fine distinctions, building up an argument and applying that to examples.

Worked Questions

Below are a few examples of how to start breaking down an interview question, complete with model answers.

Q1: In a society of angels, is the law necessary?

Applicant: Well, an angel could be defined as someone who is always inclined to do what is good, just, and moral in any situation. If I thought that the sole purpose of the law was always to achieve what is good, just, and moral, I might conclude that in a society of such creatures, law would not be necessary as angels would already be achieving this goal on their own. Why don't I continue by giving my own definition of the purpose of the law in society, taking account of the law's function as a social coordinator and as an international arbitrator? Perhaps I should also add a brief of what it means for something to be necessary and apply that definition to my discussion at hand. I may even expand this discussion further and think about what a society without any laws would look like, or indeed, if such a society would be at all possible.

This shows that **the question can be broken down into sub-parts**, which can be dealt with in turn. At this point, the interviewer can give feedback and help make any modifications necessary. In the case of the above interview, the applicant will realise that the function of the law is not just to promote what is good, just, and moral, but also to act as a method of social cohesion. The details are unimportant, but the general idea of breaking down the question into manageable parts is important. The interviewer is not looking for an expert of legal philosophy, but someone who can problem-solve in the face of new ideas.

A **poor applicant** may take a number of approaches unlikely to impress the interviewer. The first and most obvious of these is to say "I don't know anything about societies of angels" and make no attempt to move forward.

The applicants who have done this only make it worse for themselves by resisting prodding as the interviewer attempts to pull an answer from them, saying "Fine, but I'm not going to know the answer because I don't know anything about this", or equally unenthusiastic and uncooperative responses. Another approach which is unhelpful in the interview is the 'brain dump', where instead of engaging with the question, the applicant attempts to impress or distract with an assortment of related facts: "Angels would not murder each other.

Murder is a crime which can be split into two constituent parts of *mens rea* and *actus reus*, both of which are necessary for the commission of the crime. The terms *actus reus* and *mens rea* developed in English Law are derived from the principle stated by Edward Coke, namely, '*actus non facit reum nisi mens sit rea*'. This is not nearly as impressive as a more reasoned response, but the interview could be salvaged by taking feedback from the interviewer. Many of these facts could start a productive discussion which leads to the answer if the applicant listens carefully.

Q2: What is best: a written or non-written constitution?

This question is looking to see if you understand something of the nature of the **British constitution** and whether you can lay down pros and cons of an argument, with a conclusion that comes down on one side or the other of the debate.

Perhaps begin by defining what is meant by a written and a non-written constitution and try to give examples of countries with each (e.g. the UK and the USA). A constitution could be defined as a legal contract which states the terms and conditions under which a society agrees to govern itself, outlining the functions, powers and duties of the various institutions of government, regulates the relationship between them, and defines the relationship between the state and the public.

Problems of a non-written or uncodified constitution – firstly, it is difficult to know what the state of the constitution actually is, and secondly, it suggests that it is easier to make changes to the UK constitution than in countries with written constitutions, because the latter have documents with a 'higher law' status against which ordinary statute law and government action can be tested. Is the problem then more with the perception of our constitution than the legal status of the constitution itself?

Are they really so different? The American constitution may be elegantly written and succinct, but it can be amended or reinterpreted or even broken as the times demand, in the same way that the UK's unwritten constitution can be. Furthermore, even a written constitution is supplemented by unwritten conventions and most countries' constitutions embody a mixture of the two. This line of argument could lead you to conclude that the issue here is really only with semantics as **there isn't any real difference in governance**.

This question could lead to a discussion of the ways the UK constitution allows for laws to be made – e.g. "should judges have a legislative role?"

A poor applicant would not attempt to address both written and non-written constitutions, instead, sticking staunchly to whatever they have read on either subject.

Q3: What is the difference between intention and foresight?

The question is looking for your ability to give **accurate definitions of two principals central to criminal law**. Intention could be defined as an aim or a plan, whilst foresight could be defined as the ability to predict what will happen. Thinking about the way these subtly different definitions might be applied in a legal context, we see that one might foresee that doing X will lead to the death of B but that consequence was not necessarily intended.

This intuitive distinction is mirrored in **criminal law in the UK.** There are two different types of intention: direct intent which exists where the defendant embarks upon a course of conduct to bring about a result which in fact occurs, and oblique intent which exists where the defendant embarks on a course of conduct to bring about a desired result, knowing that the consequence of his actions will also bring about another result.

A particularly topical example of the application of this distinction in practice can be seen discussing "**the doctrine of double effect**". This doctrine is only really applied in medical cases. Consider this example – a doctor who administers a lethal dose of painkillers to their terminally ill patient in order to relieve their suffering also foresees that such a dose will kill the patient. Should this doctor be guilty of the murder of her patient? Ultimately, the doctrine says that if doing something morally good has a morally bad side-effect it's ethically OK to do it providing the bad side-effect wasn't intended. This is true even if you foresaw that the bad effect would probably happen.

A **poor applicant** would fail to distinguish the two and would fail to see how these definitions are applied in modern criminal law.

Q4: Does a computer have a conscience?

Intuitively, we want to answer this question with a resounding "no" as it seems obvious that only living things can have consciences. Computers are creations of man and therefore merely act according to our needs, having little or no agency of their own. A poor applicant would only be able to articulate this very basic intuitive response and would be incapable of digging further.

In fact, **the answer depends entirely upon which definitions you choose to give to the key terms** in the question. Conscience could be defined as a moral sense of right and wrong which is viewed as acting to a guide of one's behaviour.

A computer is an electronic device which is capable of receiving information and performing a sequence of operations in accordance with a predetermined set of variables. Given these two definitions, it could be possible to program a computer with a conscience.

You could discuss the **distinction between having a conscience and being 'sentient'**-the former being a form of moral compass, whilst the latter is merely the ability to perceive or feel external stimulus. Do you think "artificial intelligence" is possible? Is it dangerous? If a computer does have a conscience, what might this mean for data protection laws? Freedom of expression? Ownership? Would this mean that computers should have rules protecting them from abuse, e.g. Computer Rights?

Q5: What is justice?

It might be good to begin with a succinct **definition of 'justice'** like 'behaviour or treatment which are just' with 'just' meaning 'equitable, fair and even-handed'.

You might then want to expand on this initial definition. Perhaps an exploration of what justice means in the context of criminal law which might go as follows:

Firstly, custodial sentences are used for their deterrent effect. Secondly, decisions on the form and duration of the sentence focus upon the crime itself rather than looking at how the punishment will best rehabilitate the offender, appease the victim, and benefit society as a whole. This judicial inflexibility which we see in the sentencing of criminals reflects a right-wing conception of justice based on the maxim 'an eye for an eye'.

You might put forward that an alternative conception of justice might achieve fairer results - perhaps one which takes a **utilitarian approach** to punishment. Such a conception would necessitate finding the best possible outcome for the largest number of people.

However, the counter argument to this would be that this approach would not allow for the idea of **'moral forfeiture'**, the principle that in committing a crime, you give up some of your rights. This contextual approach gives us a taste of just how difficult it really is to define justice, even in such a narrow context.

We often hear the term **'social justice'** which is another context in which the term is applied. The concept in this context is very difficult to reconcile with justice as vengeance in the criminal context. Social justice too has several definitions; one might be socioeconomic equality amongst all members of any given society, whilst another might be more meritocratic and insist upon greater social mobility and fairness in general. We see that, upon examining this wider application of the idea of justice to non-criminal contexts, that the conception of justice itself is made even more difficult to define.

To conclude, we have proven that our initial definition of justice was not sufficient. The concept seems to defy any coherent definition as it is so broad and subjective.

Q6: Should the aim of the law be to make people happy?

One might argue that the aim of the law is to generally make everyone's lives better. Indeed, improving the quality of citizens' lives is the explicit focus of much of the policymaking and regulatory work done by many governments around the world. If we accept this, the next question would be 'what does better really mean?' One account could be that to make someone's life "better" we should render that person more able to get what they want. Another account might be that the quality of someone's life depends on the extent to which they do well at the things that are characteristically human to do. This difficulty in defining what it might be to make any one person's life better and therefore making them happy is one difficulty with placing this as the law's overarching aim – happiness is internal – how can we accurately know what anyone is feeling, and therefore truly know how well the law is working?

Perhaps one way to combat this problem could be to develop a **method of measuring subjective happiness** – a type of well-being analysis. How might we do this? Well, we could introduce a system of weekly online surveys which would be answered by a representative portion of society on how happy they were able to make particular administrative decisions. Over time, such large masses of data would allow us to accurately pinpoint just what really makes people happier and just how the law can shape itself to better achieve this.

Q7: Which laws are broken most frequently? Are they still laws?

Millions of people who declare themselves law-abiding citizens actually commit seven crimes on average per week. The most common offences are things like speeding, texting while driving, dropping litter, downloading music illegally, or riding bicycles on the pavement. Many of these more common 'minor crimes' are committed so regularly that they have almost become legal, which might be the reason so many people aren't fazed when they do break these laws.

Are these 'minor laws' still laws? You might argue that a law is a law even if it's not followed. The definition of a law, as a law, lies in the process by which it is enacted, i.e. the legislative process. This line of argument would lead you to believe that all laws are of the same importance because they become law by the same process.

However, you might not necessarily think that is the case. For instance, most people would think that killing someone would be much worse than accidentally dropping your train ticket and therefore littering. This would suggest that there is a hierarchy of laws, and therefore, that some laws are more important or that some laws are more immoral. This would lead you to conclude that 'minor laws' are still laws, but merely a lower class of laws, perhaps because the repercussions of infringement in these cases is lesser or the infringement is seen as less immoral and therefore are less thoroughly enforced.

Q8: After you have been to the hairdressers and had all of your hair cut off, do you still own your hair?

Intuitively, we believe that when our hair is attached to our heads, we do own it. The law supports this and if someone were to cut off your hair without your consent, you would be entitled to compensation.

However, where you have **consented to your hair being cut** off, the situation is very different and there is very little precedent to go on. You might argue that if you hadn't expressed an interest in maintaining your ownership of your hair once it had been cut off, it would be for the hairdresser to dispose of as he saw fit, in line with common practice in a hairdressers. You might think that the hairdresser's use of your hair would be of no consequence to you, but what if he sold it on eBay? What if it was used in an art exhibition to make a political point with which you disagreed? Would you then have a claim to your hair in these cases?

This question might lead on to a discussion about whether or not we own our own bodies. Surprisingly perhaps, we **have no legal right to decide what happens to us when we die** – instead, we can only express preferences and there are some things that the law will not let us do (e.g. leave your body to be used as meat for the dogs in Battersea Dogs' Home). We may contrast this with the approach the law takes to our other possessions after we die – in the case of all other property, your wishes are absolute. This contrast would suggest that we do not have the same legal relationship with our bodies as we do with our toasters, our cars, or our pocket-watches- but the really interesting question is – *should we?*

Q9: Should prisoners have the right to vote?

The **European Court of Human Rights** has ruled that Britain's blanket ban on voting for all convicted prisoners is a breach of their human rights. Allowing only some prisoners to vote would be ok, states the Court, but refusing the vote to all convicted prisoners is unacceptable.

Prison is generally considered to serve three key purposes; 1) to protect the public, 2) to serve as a deterrent, 3) to rehabilitate. Most prisoners have not committed crimes that warrant a life sentence. Most will eventually be released from prison. It's in everyone's interest that once out of prison, they do not commit any further crimes, but instead, become useful members of society. That involves reform whilst still in prison, and rehabilitating offenders to think - and act - more positively about their civic duties and responsibilities. One of the most important contributions a citizen can make to society is to take part in democracy and vote – removing a prisoner's civic duty does not, therefore, seem to accord with the aims of putting them in prison in the first place.

Alternatively, one might argue that all citizens of a country have implicitly agreed on a set of rules that gives them, and those around them, certain rights. It is the duty of every citizen to protect this framework and to respect the rights of others. If a person is in prison, it is because he/she broke the rules, and hence, in a way, forfeited his/her rights. The citizenship of prisoners can be seen as temporarily suspended along with all their rights.

Human rights do not mean that someone cannot be suitably punished or imprisoned for a crime once fairly tried and convicted. Human rights means that all humans deserve that society, and the State protects them from abuse of their basic civil rights. If the State can be allowed to abuse humans – any humans, for any reasons or excuses – then how can we justify laws against humans abusing other humans? How the State behaves must be reflective on how we want all humans to behave.

Human rights are meant to be universal, which means the rights apply to all humans without exception; to you and to me; even to criminals and foreigners, and even to those humans we do not like. Once we take basic rights away from one human, we start to erode the basic protections for all humans.

For 20 more worked interview questions check the *Ultimate Oxbridge Interview Guide*– flick to the back to get a free copy.

FINAL INTERVIEW ADVICE

Some DOs:

✓ **DO** speak freely about what you are thinking and ask for clarifications
✓ **DO** take suggestions and listen for pointers from your interviewer
✓ **DO** try your best to get to the answer
✓ **DO** have confidence in yourself and the abilities that got you this far
✓ **DO** a dress rehearsal beforehand so that you can identify any clothing issues before the big day
✓ **DO** make many suggestions and have many ideas
✓ **DO** take your time in answering to make sure your words come out right
✓ **DO** be polite and honest with your interviewer
✓ **DO** prepare your answers by thinking about the questions above
✓ **DO** answer the question the interviewer asked
✓ **DO** think about strengths/experiences you may wish to highlight
✓ **DO** visit www.uniadmissions.co.uk/example-interviews to see mock video Oxbridge interviews
✓ **DO** consider attending an interview course: www.uniadmissions.co.uk/

Some DON'Ts:

✗ **DON'T** be quiet – even if you can't answer a question, how you approach the question could show the interviewer what they want to see
✗ **DON'T** be afraid to pause for a moment to gather your thoughts before answering a question. It shows confidence and will lead to a clearer answer
✗ **DON'T** give them attitude or the feeling you don't want to be there
✗ **DON'T** rehearse scripted answers to be regurgitated
✗ **DON'T** answer the question you wanted them to ask – answer the one that they did!
✗ **DON'T** lie about things you have read/done (and if you already lied in your personal statement, then read/do them before the interview!)

Interview Day

➢ Get a good night's sleep
➢ Take a shower in the morning and dress at least smart-casual. It is probably safest to turn up in a suit
➢ Get there early so you aren't late or stressed out before the interview even starts
➢ Don't worry about other candidates; be nice of course, but you are there for you. Their impressions of how their interviews went have nothing to do with what the interviewers thought or how yours will go
➢ It's okay to be nervous – they know you're nervous and understand, but try to move past it and be in the moment to get the most out of the experience
➢ Talk slowly and purposefully; avoid slang and not use expletives.
➢ Try to convey to the interviewer that you are enjoying the interview
➢ It is very difficult to predict how an interview has gone so don't be discouraged if it feels like one interview didn't go well – you may have shown the interviewers exactly what they wanted to see even if it wasn't what you wanted to see. Indeed, many people who are given an offer after their interview had felt that it had not gone well at all
➢ Once the interview is over, take a well-deserved rest and enjoy the fact that there's nothing left to do
➢ Above all, smile

Afterword

Remember that the route to success is your approach and practice. With targeted preparation and focused reading, you can dramatically boost your chances of getting that dream offer.

Work hard, never give up, and do yourself justice.

Good luck!

About *UniAdmissions*

UniAdmissions is an educational consultancy that specialises in supporting **applications to Medical School and to Oxbridge**.

Every year, we work with hundreds of applicants and schools across the UK. From free resources to our *Ultimate Guide Books* and from intensive courses to bespoke individual tuition – with a team of **300 Expert Tutors** and a proven track record, it's easy to see why *UniAdmissions* is the **UK's number one admissions company**.

To find out more about our support like intensive **courses** and **tuition**, check out **www.uniadmissions.co.uk**

Your Free Book

Thanks for purchasing this Ultimate Guide Book. Readers like you have the power to make or break a book – hopefully you found this one useful and informative. If you have time, *UniAdmissions* would love to hear about your experiences with this book.

As thanks for your time we'll send you another ebook from our Ultimate Guide series absolutely <u>FREE</u>!

How to Redeem Your Free Ebook in 3 Easy Steps

1) Find the book you have either on your Amazon purchase history

or your email receipt to help find the book on Amazon.

2) On the product page at the Customer Reviews area, click on 'Write a customer review'

Write your review and post it! Copy the review page or take a screen shot of the review you have left.

3) Head over to www.uniadmissions.co.uk/free-book and select your chosen free ebook! You can choose from:

- ✓ The Ultimate LNAT Guide – 400 Practice Questions
- ✓ The Ultimate Oxbridge Interview Guide
- ✓ The Ultimate UCAS Personal Statement Guide
- ✓ The Ultimate Law School Application Guide
- ✓ The Ultimate Cambridge Law Test Guide
- ✓ LNAT Mock Papers

Your ebook will then be emailed to you – it's as simple as that!

Alternatively, you can buy all the above titles at **www.uniadmissions.co.uk/our-books**

LNAT Online Course

If you're looking to improve your LNAT score in a short space of time, our **LNAT Online Course** is perfect for you. The LNAT Online Course offers all the content of a traditional course in a single easy-to-use online package-available instantly after checkout. The online videos are just like the classroom course, ready to watch and re-watch at home or on the go and all with our expect Oxbridge tuition and advice.

You'll get full access to all our LNAT resources including:

✓ Copy of our acclaimed book "The Ultimate LNAT Guide"
✓ Full access to extensive LNAT online resources including:
✓ 4 complete mock papers
✓ 400 practice questions
✓ 10 hours Online on-demand lecture series
✓ Ongoing Tutor Support until Test date – never be alone again.

The course is normally £99 but you can get **£ 20 off** by using the code *"UAONLINE20"* at checkout.

https://www.uniadmissions.co.uk/product/lnat-online-course/

£20 VOUCHER:

UAONLINE20